HIRING SUCCESS

HIRING
SUCCESS

HOW VISIONARY CEOS
COMPETE FOR
THE BEST TALENT

JEROME
TERNYNCK

LIONCREST
PUBLISHING

HIRING SUCCESS
How Visionary CEOs Compete for the Best Talent

ISBN   978-1-5445-0690-6   *Hardcover*
       978-1-5445-0689-0   *Paperback*
       978-1-5445-0688-3   *Ebook*

For my parents, who let me be myself.

For my daughters, who make me better.

For the Smartians, who have joined me on a quest to connect people to jobs at scale.

For all the recruiters out there, making a difference every day.

For the millions of people in search of their dream job.

TABLE OF CONTENTS

PART THREE: THE ART (AND SCIENCE) OF SELECTION

PART FOUR: HIRING SUCCESS AT SCALE

INTRODUCTION

Several years ago, at a who's-who-in-Silicon-Valley dinner hosted by Marc Benioff of Salesforce, I got to talking with some fellow executives about my favorite topic, recruiting. A bank CEO seated next to me asked about my company, SmartRecruiters, and I explained that our software helps businesses find and hire top talent at scale.

"That's great," the guy said. "You've tapped into something absolutely critical: hiring amazing talent."

"Are you hiring amazing talent?" I asked.

"Well, of course—at least I think so," the CEO responded. "My human resources team takes care of that."

"How is it working out?"

"I guess it's fine," he said. "We're hiring people."

I pointed out that hiring people and hiring *great* people were not the same.

"Are you hiring the people that Goldman Sachs rejected?" I asked the CEO. "Or are you actually competing for the best talent in your market?"

The executive pushed back his chair, looking uncomfortable. "Tell me more about what you do," he said.

As I explained that I help businesses transform by treating recruiting as a sales and marketing function, not a back-office function, I saw his dawning realization: What if I'm not competing for the best talent?

Like many busy executives, the CEO believed that hiring top talent was a high priority, but without a formula to ensure that he was actually achieving that goal, he had been dropping the ball. And he's not alone. Over 80 percent of Fortune 500 companies say they are not hiring the best talent.[1]

Unfortunately, most companies lump recruiting in with menial human resources tasks like processing payroll or vacation

---

1   McKinsey & Company, 2012.

requests. But this is not a process to be automated and forgotten about. There is a global competition for the best talent. And sooner or later, leaders who don't realize this will find their companies put out of business by competitors who do.

So, how do you ensure that your organization is hiring amazing talent? I'm going to share the answer to that question in the pages that follow.

But first, how did I discover the recipe for hiring success?

My passion for hiring was born in the military. In 1992, I was twenty-two and serving my mandatory two years of service in the French Army. I'd spent the first part of my tenure training at École spéciale militaire de Saint-Cyr (Saint-Cyr—the equivalent of West Point), then joined the paratroopers as a lieutenant. I was in charge of training the incoming newcomers, who came to my base by the busload—a new batch every sixty days. I quickly learned to identify which recruits were suited for which posts. It wasn't just about who could run fast or shoot well; it was about who was a team player, who was a born leader. Every sixty days, I'd dispatch my charges, now trained soldiers, to their various stations and start all over again training the next batch.

After completing my service, I set out to the Czech Republic in search of opportunity. The Berlin Wall had just fallen, and the

Eastern Bloc was opening up for business. It was like a reset of the entire country. It was incredibly exciting to me: though I had no money and no clue what profession to pursue, I had an entrepreneurial spirit. Sensing that inspiration would find me in bustling Prague, I settled there, asking everyone I met, "What's needed here? What kind of company should I start?" The answer almost always came in two parts:

Part one: "Any business you can think of, we need it in Prague! The possibilities are limitless!"

Part two: "But good luck finding great people to work for you."

Finding specialized talent was a major problem because the economy was transitioning from a communist, centralized economy into a liberal, capitalist one. If you were looking for someone with five years' experience in marketing, nobody in the country qualified, because five years earlier marketing hadn't existed there. This was true in so many fields.

MY FIRST AHA MOMENT

It didn't take long for it to hit me: the businesses fueling Prague's boom depended on their ability to hire talent. Seizing the opportunity before me, I opened one of the first recruitment agencies in the country. Right away, it was clear that I'd been correct: the many Western companies now setting up shop in the Czech Republic really did need help. Long accustomed to hiring for aptitude (the candidate's past experience or education), not attitude (the candidate's personality and potential), they were terrible at identifying raw talent. Which of course was exactly what they needed to be doing in order to bridge the gap between available specialized jobs and Prague's inexperienced talent pool. So, I jumped in and helped companies like L'Oréal, McDonald's, and Microsoft fill thousands of positions. It was a very democratic and diverse process; almost anyone could claim any job if they had the right characteristics and attitude for it.

Over the next seven years, my recruitment agency expanded throughout Central and Eastern Europe, opening offices in seven countries. Then came the internet in the late nineties— and with it, limitless opportunities for recruiters. No longer did we need to sort through stacks of paper resumes to find candidates; the process could be automated online. I moved to London and founded a recruiting software company.

The first software I built was an applicant tracking system (ATS) that launched in 2002. My software, like its competitors', put candidates into a database that automatically tracked every stage of their application process. ATS software was so cost-effective and efficient at processing job applicants that 95 percent of Fortune 500 companies soon adopted some form of it.

By 2010, when the ATS market was nearing $2 billion world-wide, I sold my software company and set off for San Francisco on a mission to try to create something new and better.

Because, while my software had been successful, I knew I hadn't yet achieved my mission.

A NEW MISSION TO REDUCE SEARCH FRICTION

At the time, the United States was still reeling from the after-effects of the 2008 financial crisis. Unemployment was high, the economy was down, and people were struggling to make ends meet. I wanted to be part of the solution. I wanted to help solve unemployment by giving companies the tools to find the talent they needed to succeed.

What had been missing from early ATS software, mine included, was a crucial piece of the puzzle: these systems filled the role of tracking candidates, but they didn't help companies attract those candidates. They didn't solve the problem of search friction.

At the time, the concept of search friction—how long it takes for supply and demand to meet in the job market—was relatively new. It was coined by three professors—Dale Mortensen, Christopher Pissarides, and Peter Diamond—who won the 2010 Nobel Prize for economics for their work studying the problem of unemployment, and what to do about it. The scholars had found that high search friction in the labor market was very bad for the economy. How bad? It was, and still is, a global problem costing us trillions of dollars each year.[2]

In San Francisco, I began studying companies that were already successfully using technology to reduce search friction. The rental market was a brilliant example: thanks to Airbnb, for instance, you no longer had to conduct weeks of research to find an apartment for a weekend on the other side of the world. Instead, you could book a place with two clicks. Friction in that market had been removed.

I wanted to do the same thing for the recruiting market. And I knew this meant that in addition to offering outward-bound recruiting tools, this new product must not treat hiring like a rote process. Candidates deserved better than to be moved through the interviewing and hiring experience like widgets on a factory assembly line. They were humans, not products, after all. And they were *vital to the economic well-being of the nation and the world. Shouldn't they be treated with due respect?*

One day, I took a blank sheet of paper and wrote down what it would take for a recruiting software platform to hire amazing talent on scale. I zeroed in on three core attributes:

---

2   McKinsey & Company, 2012.

- Candidate experience: It should help me find candidates.

- Hiring manager engagement: It should help me pick the right talent, engaging both recruiters and hiring managers.

- Recruiter productivity: It should increase productivity by containing all of my data in one place.

These became the three principles of hiring success, woven into what became the SmartRecruiters platform.

After four years of development and testing, my team and I launched the first version of our software in January 2015. Since then, we have acquired 700 clients around the world, including Visa, Bosch, Ikea, LinkedIn, and Twitter. Today, our platform facilitates over a hundred thousand interviews monthly, and we just celebrated our one-millionth-hire mark. We're proud that many of our customers have *doubled* their hiring velocity—the percentage of jobs filled on time.

Most importantly, our software makes applying for jobs easier and more fun for candidates, while simultaneously attracting the highest quality candidates. How do we know this? We created a formula that measures the fit between new hires and jobs, not just the quantity.

Now, my mission is to give every company the tools they need to achieve this level of hiring success. And I want to give every candidate a job they love.

ARE YOU READY FOR HIRING SUCCESS?

This book reveals my tested strategy for hiring amazing talent and out-hiring the competition. I didn't write it for recruiters. Nor for those interested in tips and tricks for hiring. Our goal at SmartRecruiters is to help companies hire amazing talent at scale. Which is why I've written this book for the executive who has *significant* power to change the way recruiting is done at their company—but until now has lacked the right strategy and tools.

This book is for the CEO I met at that Silicon Valley party three years ago—the one who said hiring great talent was his top priority but didn't know how to get his team to execute on that vision. It's for the disruptors of the world who are ready to shake up and transform the recruitment process at their companies. It's for leaders who understand the fundamental truth that the company with the best talent wins. It's for executives, leaders, and managers who want to build an A-team. It's for you.

PART ONE

YOU ARE
WHO YOU HIRE

CHAPTER 1

THE WAR FOR TALENT

The single biggest constraint on the success of my organization is the ability to get and to hang on to enough of the right people.

—Jim Collins, *Good to Great: Why Some Companies Make the Leap...and Others Don't*

To build a strong business, you need three things: ideas, money, and talent. Look around you: there's no shortage of money or ideas. In our free-market economy, access to business capital has long been readily available, and there can be no doubt that we live in an age of unprecedented acceleration, discovery, and progress. As for available talent to drive all this growth? That's another story.

In a milestone 1997 employment study, Steven Hankin of McKinsey & Company declared that the "war for talent" would be a defining challenge for twenty-first-century businesses. In the heyday of the first dot com boom, Hankin's prediction gained widespread notice—but then the dot com bubble burst, the Great Recession hit, and joblessness soared. When the unemployment rate hit nearly 10 percent in 2009, many assumed that the war for talent was over.

Far from it. By 2015, unemployment was cut in half, and the war for talent raged once again. Today, recruiters joke that if the war is over, it's because the candidates have won.

WHAT'S FUELING THIS WAR?

SPECIALIZED JOBS ARE CREATING A SKILLS GAP

When Homo sapiens first walked the earth, there were two jobs: hunter and gatherer. Century by century, our work has evolved. Whereas our great-great-grandfathers' career options included lumberjack, farmer, herder, and a dozen or so others, teenagers today will choose from over eleven million possible jobs when they enter the workforce. And first graders? The majority of their job options haven't even been invented yet, but it's safe to say that their skillsets will be exponentially more sophisticated than the ones we employ today.[3]

Twenty years ago, a software developer was a software developer was a software developer. Now, an iOS software developer building mobile apps on the Apple platform has a completely different skillset from the developer building for the Android on the Google platform. And within those two platforms alone, expertise runs the gamut from front-end to back-end to middle-tier to full-stack to desktop to mobile to graphics to Dev Ops to security, and on and on…

The stark reality is that the tech boom is causing employee shortages in *every* sector of the job market. As industries in every corner of the marketplace adopt new technologies, they must hire specialized employees to support that tech. When specialization increases, the pool of potential talent decreases. It becomes nearly impossible to have enough of the right talent to fuel growth.

According to one assessment, demand for skilled workers will surpass supply in 2030 by over eighty-five million.[4] If you quantify this potential talent shortage, the financial impact will be more than 8 trillion in unrealized annual

---

3   LinkedIn, 2017.
4   Korn/Ferry International, 2008.

revenue. For reference, that's the current GDP of Japan and Germany combined.

This is not a localized problem. All countries, with the noticeable exception of India—the only country to forecast a 2030 skilled talent surplus—will be affected for the foreseeable future. McKinsey's experts calculate that employers in Europe and North America already require eighteen million more college-educated workers than are available today.

And it's not just a shortage in college-educated workers; developing economies worldwide are grappling to fill a combined forty-five million unfilled jobs designed for employees with secondary school education and vocational training. Simply put, there's just not enough talent for everyone. Therefore, company leaders need to adjust their mentality now—or prepare to lose out in the war for talent.

TENURE IS DROPPING

Not only is it harder to find and hire people with the right skills; it's getting harder to keep them. Gone are the days of IBM and Procter and Gamble lifers, retiring after thirty years of loyal service with well-earned company pensions. The Bureau of Labor Statistics now reports that U.S. workers remain at each job on average about four-and-a-half years. For younger workers, it's half that.

The consequence boils down to simple math. A company of ten thousand employees with an average tenure of two years is hiring close to five thousand people a year, just to stay afloat— essentially changing up half of its staff every year.

Why do so many employees get restless and move on? It's not necessarily about their pay. In Silicon Valley, it's common to see an intern from Stanford make $45,000 for the summer, or a software developer with a few years' experience making as much as $500,000 a year. It's also not about the perks. Facebook and Google, for example, offer a long list of amenities including laundry, dry cleaning, childcare, and massages—yet the average employee tenure at Facebook is two-and-a-half years.

You may tell yourself that these trends don't apply to *your* company—that your employees are happy where they are. But don't be so sure. In a recent survey by McKinsey Global Institute, nearly three-quarters of employees said they were thinking about another job. Why wouldn't yours be, too?

So, more likely, you're sitting on a time bomb—fighting to get and keep talent while your competition is becoming more and more aggressive at trying to steal that talent from you. And all the while, there's another disruptive trend you need to be aware of: contingent workers.

THE GIG ECONOMY IS BOOMING

Contract work is on the rise, with nearly fifty-seven million Americans now freelancing.[5] Google's contract employees, for example, make up over half of their total workforce. Historically, this might have been good for companies, because leveraging freelancing reduces costs and gives companies flexibility, right?

True, but more recently, employees with high-demand skills have been leveraging the model of contract work to *their* benefit, by demanding increased flexibility and higher than full-time rates. They contract with several customers, rather than commit, and find that the benefits of forgoing old-fashioned employment—better pay, work-life balance, interesting projects, and remote work—outweigh the risks.

I know one Montreal-based entrepreneur who's built a booming business brokering contracts between big tech companies and some of the most expensive guns for hire in the world: expert open source software developers. This group of talent is highly sought after—flooded with top-tier, full-time offers every month. Despite this, they choose to stay independent contractors. The power really is in their hands, folks.

---

5   Upwork, 2019.

THE RISE OF REMOTE

One of my friends, a top data scientist, makes more money than I do working in between surf sessions from his "office" on the beach in Costa Rica. Another fellow entrepreneur runs a successful software business with five hundred employees all working remotely without a single office around the world.

Gone are the days when companies were relegated to hiring exclusively from the local talent pool. With collaboration software like Slack, Zoom, and endless others to support it, the modern workforce is as productive as it is disparate. According to LinkedIn, the number of job posts mentioning "work flexibility" has jumped by 78 percent since 2016.

Companies *not* onboard with remote work are at a competitive disadvantage, missing out on a recruiting playground that's become national, often global. If the talent is global, then your recruiting should be, too! The best candidates for your U.S. company may be sitting in Zimbabwe, Costa Rica, or the Ukraine. Should you hire them? If they have good internet access, the answer is probably yes.

WHO WILL WIN THE WAR FOR TALENT?

So you see, we have a perfect storm. It's not just one trend, but the convergence of several that's dramatically changing today's job market. In the talent economy, the business with the best talent wins, period. The question is: Will *your* company win the best talent, or be out-hired by the competition? It's up to you.

KEY TAKEAWAYS

- In the talent economy, the business with the best talent wins, period.

- Driven by increased job complexity, skills gap, dropping tenure, and globalization, the war for talent is intensifying.

- Competition for talent is now a real threat to business success and a top priority for CEOs.

- Smart businesses need to invest in hiring success, or risk being out-hired by their competitors.

CHAPTER 2

YOU ARE
WHO YOU HIRE

*The secret of my success is that we have gone to
exceptional lengths to hire the best people in the world.*

—Steve Jobs

THE RONALDO EFFECT

As president of the Italian football club Juventus, Andrea
Agnelli gambled $112 million to sign the thirty-three-
year-old soccer star Cristiano Ronaldo in 2018. It was
quite the financial risk, four times more costly than any other
contract in the division. But Agnelli's bet paid off. The charis-
matic new player was an asset on *and* off the field, attracting a
massive global fan base, jump-starting the club's social media

accounts with ten million new followers, and selling out stadiums from game one. Coined the "Ronaldo Effect" by investors, the star player's impact on Juventus's bottom line was staggering. By July 2018, a few months after Ronaldo's acquisition, the club's share price had more than doubled.[6]

In sports, it's very clear that who you have on your team defines everything. And guess what? In business, it's the same. Who you hire across every specialty, from top to bottom, defines your ability to compete, and it defines *you* as a leader. The best leaders attract the best talent. And talent is the key to success.

This isn't just lofty talk. Research shows that in very high-complexity occupations, superior employees are up to 800 percent more productive than their peers. The productivity gap for high-complexity employees is large as well but drops to 125 percent. For medium and low complexity workers, the gap is still significant, at 85 and 50 percent higher productivity, respectively. Across roles, from senior data scientists at Google, to burger flippers at McDonald's, the relationship between caliber of talent and business performance should not be underestimated.

Let's bring this closer to home. Suppose your business strategy involves cross-functional initiatives that, based on current

---

6   Business Insider, 2018.

metrics, will take three years to complete. Imagine taking 20 percent of your average workers and replacing them with great talent. How soon would you achieve the desired impact? If your new, superior hires were 400 percent more productive, your end goal would take less than two years instead of three. If the new workers were very highly skilled, with 800 percent greater productivity, your three-year project would wrap in less than one year.

Now, imagine you decide to stick with the talent you've got—they're "good enough." Meanwhile, your competitor replaces 20 percent of their workforce with superior talent. What happens? The competitor beats you to market by a year, maybe two.

How you compete for talent defines how you compete as a business. Take Google, one of the greatest talent magnets out there. Yes, they have an amazing search engine monopoly that generates massive revenues and profits. But equally, Google has a perfectly tuned recruiting process, which they heavily invest in. Google has eight times more recruiters, per employee, than the average Fortune 500 company—meaning they out-invest their competitors by a multiple of eight on recruiter headcount alone.[7] Are you surprised that they have the best talent in the world? Are you surprised they are poised to out-innovate across many different sectors?

---

7   Fortune, 2012.

What is the difference between McKinsey and your average consulting firm, if not the people? What about Goldman Sachs and a midsize bank? The people.

Given that hiring amazing talent is so critical, it would seem logical that all companies would focus on it. Quite the contrary: 77 percent of Fortune 500 executives believe that they actually *don't* hire great people.[8]

Let's talk about why, and what you can do about it.

RECRUITING TODAY IS BROKEN

Mediocrity will never do. You are
capable of something better.
—Gordon B. Hinckley

What's the precise problem in recruiting today? Is it a sourcing problem (we can't find the right candidates)? Is it a leadership problem (we don't clearly define the role and talent needed)? A selection problem (we don't assess and evaluate the right people)? Or a processing problem (we lack the right technology)? In today's complex world, it's a mix of all of the above.

---

8   PwC, 2017.

Recruiting used to be so simple. A hundred years ago, companies would create a job, post it outside of their factory, and evaluate candidates who showed up at their door. This worked because jobs were not very complicated; the skills and talent needed were not as developed as they are today. So, everything was fast.

Gradually—and then quickly—the world changed. The biggest change in modern history is of course the internet, which turned recruiting into an online function. Companies adjusted by investing in applicant tracking systems (ATS) to automate and manage the process. Many subpar tracking systems are still used today despite the fact that they leave candidates frustrated and unhappy. Who wouldn't be? On average, applicants must now compete with two hundred other job seekers for any position they seek.

At the same time, most recruiting functions are still being measured through time-to-fill and cost-per-hire—faster and cheaper metrics that drive a race to the bottom. HR leaders are not empowered to ask their CEOs for an increase in cost-per-hire—even though it's proven that top talent can be up to 800 percent more productive than mediocre talent. Seems like a compelling ROI to me.

As a direct result of the automation created by applicant tracking systems, companies have gradually lost the skills necessary for recruiting. Over 50 percent of CEOs now outsource this core competency to a third party—essentially throwing money at the problem.

United States companies spend $20 million to fill sixty-six million jobs annually, with the majority going to hiring. That's an average of just over $4,000 per job placement.[9] And yet, they're still not succeeding.

SmartRecruiters recently ran a net hiring score (NHS) survey to measure quality of hire at a large U.S. technology company. The survey questioned both hiring managers and new employees ninety days post-hire, asking them: "On a scale of zero to ten: How much of a fit is this new hire/job for you?" More than half of the time, either the new hire, the manager, or both said they were underwhelmed with their decision.

Imagine being in the shoes of the CEO who has just learned that over half of her hires were essentially mistakes. As she would well realize, the impact on her company's culture, morale, and outright performance would be deep. And she, of course, would bear the long-term consequences when those employees left for greener pastures—as statistics predict they would.

First-year employee turnover in the United States has reached unprecedented levels, according to a 2018 study by Work

9   The Society for Human Resource Management, 2018.

Institute. Over the last eight years, the number of workers choosing to quit their jobs has grown steadily. If recent trends continue, one in three workers—forty-eight million employees—will quit in 2020.10 And while their top talent will move on, the company that can't compete will be stuck with the under-performing employees who have nowhere else to go.

CALCULATING THE IMPACT OF HIRING MISTAKES

What's the real price of poor hiring practices? Glassdoor estimates an average yearly cost of more than $53,000 per unfilled job openings across all sectors. The technology market is suffering the most—losing $20 billion to unfilled jobs every year[11]—due to the high scarcity of specialized talent. Because these costs are not easily quantifiable, they often go overlooked. But complacency is expensive. Unfilled jobs do not save money in unpaid salaries and benefits, but rather cost your company across the board.

When it comes to replacing bad hires, the cost is at least 30 percent of the annual salary for the position. Why so high? You must factor in lost productivity from the vacant position and the cost of recruiting, hiring, and onboarding the

---

10 Bureau of Labor Statistics, 2018.
11 Forbes Technology Council, 2017.

replacement. Now, let's say you make a bad hire, but the person sticks around, and you choose not to replace them. Here's where the costs compound and create a ripple effect. When you hire someone mediocre, not only are they less productive, but they also create an unhealthy work environment, which in turn lowers morale and productivity.

And it's probably even worse than you think. Take Pareto's 80/20 Rule, for example. That's the theory that 20 percent of action drives 80 percent of results. Burdening the top 20 percent of workers with subpar teammates signals that you don't require and value high performance.

In short, introducing mediocre hires to your company is like introducing a disease.

Thankfully, the inverse of this scenario is true as well. Businesses that excel at hiring perform over three times better.[12] Which side of the equation do you want to be on?

MY HIRING FAILURE

Two years ago, I made a costly mistake, myself. I was trying to hire a product manager to build and launch a new offering

---

12 Boston Consulting Group, 2012.

at SmartRecruiters. I had expected the product to be a big add-on to our platform, and I knew it was one that our customers wanted and expected. So, we talked ourselves into hiring a candidate with an excellent aptitude and experience level, despite initial concerns about their attitude and personality. We compromised, ignoring our own rule: always hire for attitude, not aptitude. After the six-figure hire was onboarded, they set off to design the new offering with an excellent engineering team in place. Three months later, however, we realized that this person was not a fit for the role, despite their long, successful career history. The product was not designed to interact well with the rest of our platform, and we needed to start over from scratch.

Imagine my frustration. It took us about two months to find a good replacement and another three months before this person was onboarded. We missed our scheduled launch at our annual Hiring Success conference, where over a thousand heads of talent acquisition, most of them customers, convene. All-in-all, the product launch was delayed by an entire year. Based on how successful the offering ultimately turned out to be, I believe that single hiring mistake cost us over $1 million in revenue.

Now, add in the accrued salary and onboarding costs of this failed hire—another $80,000 down the drain—and top that off with the cost of replacing the employee, and you can see how quickly this adds up. Then there are the less quantifiable impacts, including the morale of the troops, or engineers, who were frustrated by the wasted work effort. Plus, the disappointment of our customers. A disaster all around. There is an upside to my story, though…

DON'T COMPROMISE ON HIRING SUCCESS

The failure I just described inspired me to make a promise to myself: I would never again compromise *one iota* on hiring success. I feel good about my odds of keeping that promise. How can I be so confident? Because I know that capturing the very best talent really is as easy as one, two, three:

1. Attract enough great candidates so you are never forced to compromise.

2. Create a collaborative evaluation process that leverages the wisdom of the team.

3. Never hire a "maybe." In recruiting, a maybe is a no.

As you'll discover in the course of this book, I have much more to say about candidate attraction, the team evaluation process, and how to banish the word "maybe" from your recruiting vocabulary. For now, I'll reiterate that hiring success is not a human resources process that needs to be done fast and cheap. It's a competitive muscle that, when exercised, allows you to out-hire your competition and disrupt their business.

It's time to flip the switch. Let's think about recruiting as a sales and marketing function, and invest in it as such. That's the first concrete step toward hiring success. In the next chapter, we'll talk about the three principles behind hiring success, and how they can lift your company to new heights.

KEY TAKEAWAYS

- Who you hire defines your company, your leadership, and ultimately your ability to compete.

- However, recruiting is broken—treated as an administrative function, costing companies greatly in lost revenue and efficiency.

- Hiring success is the ability to attract, select, and hire amazing talent on time and on budget for any role.

- Smart companies understand that hiring success is business success, and they invest accordingly.

CHAPTER 3

PRINCIPLES OF HIRING SUCCESS

I n the course of my long career in recruiting, I've had the opportunity to study the hiring practices of dozens of companies. I've observed that those who are most successful at hiring the best talent excel at three core practices—or what I call the principles of hiring success:

- **Candidate experience:** It all starts with a company's ability to attract amazing talent by applying the appropriate mix of modern marketing strategies. Delivering an engaging experience for candidates at every single touchpoint throughout the recruiting process is essential for success.

- **Manager collaboration:** Companies are empowered to excel when they approach hiring as a team effort, where all relevant stakeholders are responsive and held accountable for hiring decisions. Particularly, hiring managers partner closely with their recruiting peers, because they are invested in hiring the best.

- **Recruiter productivity:** Best-in-class companies focus on recruiter productivity, allowing them to automate their function by bringing all data processes and suppliers into a single platform that supports talent acquisition end-to-end.

Let's take a closer look at what it means to practice each of those core principles.

FIRST: CANDIDATE EXPERIENCE

The candidate experience is the heart of a great recruiting strategy. It's unfortunate that many companies fail to realize this—let alone acknowledge the human element of recruiting. They neglect to craft the candidate's journey with the same thoughtfulness that they put into the customer's journey.

The secret is to think of the candidates as customers to be marketed to. In other words, good recruiting—from attracting and nurturing these ideal customer-candidates to closing the deal with a job offer—should be approached as a marketing strategy. In the following chapters, we'll explore the tools for implementing this strategy: advertising, content marketing, employee referrals, and direct sourcing. By utilizing these tools in your campaign, you'll simultaneously acquire the best talent and elevate your candidate experience and company brand. These objectives go hand in hand.

Without a proper candidate experience, however, you *will be* out-hired by your competition. When hiring managers have a mediocre pool of candidates, they compromise—making mediocre hires. The best you have is not the same as the best you can get. If you want your hiring managers to make outstanding hires, they need excellent options.

SECOND: HIRING MANAGER COLLABORATION

Hiring top talent requires a team approach. Recruiters alone cannot build a competitive team. It must be a collaboration between recruiters and hiring managers. Many companies believe it's the recruiter's job to actually hire. I disagree with this approach. It should be a manager's job to build their team and hire the best of the best. The hiring manager should be at the center of recruiting.

Companies that succeed in hiring see a great collaborative relationship between the hiring manager and the recruiters. That collaboration starts with the creation of a detailed job description to ensure that the company, not the candidate, shapes the role at hand.

Once an exemplary candidate pool has been assembled, the hiring manager and recruiter further collaborate on the interview process. Considering that approximately 50 percent of managers feel inadequately prepared to identify soft skills and assess a candidate's qualifications, team-based hiring is by far the most effective path forward.[13] To facilitate this process, I recommend creating a well-defined candidate scorecard, which allows for several things. First, it fosters conversations between the recruiter and the manager early on. What are we looking for? Who, precisely, is the ideal candidate? Second, it serves as an interview guideline—questions should be developed to match each of the criteria. Third, it provides a feedback mechanism. This form of structured, team-based feedback mixes the art of hiring—interviewing—with science. We'll discuss the hiring scorecard at length in the next chapter.

Throughout this collaborative hiring process, the recruiter is the marketer, and the manager is the salesperson. The

---

13   Harvard Business Review, 2019.

recruiter's job is to fill the pipeline with great options, and the manager's job is to close the deal.

THIRD: RECRUITER PRODUCTIVITY

Recruiting has evolved to be a high-tech, digital function. It involves at least hundreds of thousands of transactions a year. All of the data processes and suppliers need to be in one place.

Let's say you're a company of ten thousand people and you're hiring two thousand employees a year—a conservative estimate. With those kinds of numbers, you're probably going to process around three hundred thousand candidates annually. Each of these candidates needs to be reviewed, rated, and responded to. Approximately ten thousand candidates, at least, may be brought in for interviews yearly—many for several. So, in total you're organizing thirty thousand interviews every year and issuing approximately twelve hundred offer letters.

The sheer volume of activity that's happening in real time, and under high-stakes pressure, is quite staggering. If you don't give your recruiters the right infrastructure to be successful, there's no chance they will manage it. What is that infrastructure?

The ideal talent acquisition suite offers four key attributes:

1. **A robust platform:** The system should have all the functionalities to manage candidate acquisition from start to finish. It should be user-friendly and designed for collaboration between managers and recruiters.

2. **Global compliance:** A system that's global in nature is critical. It ensures international compliance with diverse regulations, including data privacy regulations to help you correctly process significant amounts of private data in recruiting.

3. **Ecosystem connections:** The system will seamlessly connect with third-party recruiting vendors such as Simply, Indeed, and LinkedIn, to name a few. It will also connect with background-check services and facilitate reference checks.

4. **Embedded intelligence:** A modern talent acquisition suite should provide embedded intelligence. It leverages artificial intelligence (AI) and machine learning to help drive efficiency in the complex job of processing and hiring thousands of candidates.

Once you have the three principles down, how is hiring success measured? Let's find out.

KEY TAKEAWAYS

- Recruiting has evolved significantly in the twenty-first century. Best-in-class companies use the three principles of hiring success to out-hire their competition.

- Top companies offer an amazing candidate experience and think of recruiting as a sales and marketing function.

- They put collaboration between the recruiter and hiring manager at the center of their recruiting process.

- They leverage technology to give their recruiters A to Z support in productivity and delivering amazing results.

CHAPTER 4

MEASURING HIRING SUCCESS

L ast year, I was speaking at a recruiting conference to approximately five hundred recruiting leaders from a variety of industries. In my opening statement, I asked the audience a simple question: Who has been to a management or board meeting where they proposed to increase the cost-per-hire of new candidates? To my dismay, no one raised their hand.

If recruiting is like sales and marketing—a competitive function—then investing in recruiting should be a given, right? Instead, companies pride themselves in keeping their costs per hire low, and the quality of candidates suffers. (Taken to an extreme, you could have a cost-per-hire of zero if you hired the first jobless person you saw on the street—but then, most certainly, the candidate would be wrong for the job).

Many companies resist investing in hiring because they lack the proper metrics to show that spending more leads to better hires and better profits. Instead, they measure time-to-hire, a speed metric, and cost-per-hire, a cost metric. Recruiters take the single function their CEOs care about the most and try to deliver it faster and cheaper. But fast and cheap are not measures of hiring success. The current hiring metrics are all wrong, and it's a big problem. The good news: it's easy to solve.

A NEW FRAMEWORK FOR MEASURING HIRING SUCCESS

If you want to set your recruiting team on the path to success, then start measuring hiring success for its output. Start measuring it according to your goal of acquiring amazing talent on demand. The three main metrics of hiring success you *should* track are hiring budget, hiring velocity, and net hiring score (NHS).

THE FIRST METRIC: HIRING BUDGET

The hiring budget represents the total cost of recruiting, divided by new hire payroll. Recruiting costs include talent acquisition team salaries, program spending, candidate travel costs, technology infrastructure, and your advertising, sourcing, and marketing budget. It does not include time spent by interviewers and the hiring team as they engage in the process. In the United States, the average hiring budget is just over 7 percent.

While many companies try to rein in the cost of recruiting, forward-looking organizations consider their hiring budget an investment—just like a marketing budget—to grow their business. They express their hiring budgets relative to the salaries of the people hired, or new hire payroll (NHP). Companies may choose to allocate higher percentages to more important hires.

Organizations can invest, depending on their industry, between 5 and 15 percent of new hire payroll in their hiring budget. What should your company's hiring budget be? Well, essentially that depends on what level of quality and speed you expect. That's where the next two metrics are key: hiring velocity and net hiring score. These measurements will allow you to decide how much you want to invest in exchange for the outcomes you want.

THE SECOND METRIC: HIRING VELOCITY

Hiring velocity, the percentage of jobs filled on time, is highly correlated to business velocity. In other words, it measures a company's ability to hire the people they need when they need them, in order to meet their objectives on time. As a CEO, if the head of recruiting comes to me and happily says, "Our time-to-fill went from forty-three days to thirty-nine days," I frankly don't care. What I care about is goal attainment—that my hiring targets are aligned to what various teams need in order to perform. Hiring velocity of above 80 percent strongly indicates that your business is progressing at a healthy pace. Whether your hiring time-to-fill is 120 days or 30 days, it really doesn't matter, as long as you've aligned hiring against business goals, and delivered on time to meet those goals.

On the other hand, if you run at a hiring velocity of 50 percent—filling half your jobs on time—you will not have the capacity to complete projects on time. Imagine having only half the engineers needed to build a product, or half the salespeople needed to meet your sales budget. Obviously, hiring on time can have a significant impact on your business. However, it's actually less important than the metric most organizations rarely track, which is the quality of the people brought on board...

THE THIRD METRIC: NET HIRING SCORE

When companies attempt to measure their quality of hires, most seem to do it through year-end performance reviews. The reality: waiting a year is too late. You want to know if you're good at recruiting right now. And there is no better determinant of your hiring success than your overall net hiring score (NHS), which measures job fit. Specifically, the net hiring score, which ranges from -100 to +100, tells you whether your new hires are poor, moderate, or strong fits for your organization. Similar to the Net Promoter Score (NPS), the standard for measuring customer experience, the NHS is calculated by subtracting the percentage of poor fits (those who respond to a new hire and hiring manager survey with ratings of 0–6) from the percentage of great fits (those who respond to the survey with ratings of 9–10) and multiplying by 100. New hires should consider job description accuracy, management competency, and company culture when answering. Hiring managers should consider the new hire's aptitude, attitude, and growth potential when answering. This simple process is outlined in the graphic below.

Step 1
Ask hiring managers the following question after new hire ramp-up time: **On a scale of 0-10, how much of a fit is this new hire for the job?**

Step 2
Ask new hires the following question after ramp-up time: **On a scale of 0-10, how much of a fit is this new job for you?**

Step 3
Gather all results and categorize into the percentage of those who answered 9-10 (Strong fits) and subtract from it the percentage of those who answered 0-6 (Poor fits). Multiply this result by 100 to land on your NHS.

NHS = [**% Strong Fits** - % Poor Fits] x 100

YOUR HIRING SUCCESS SCORECARD

Now, combine your company average new hiring score with your hiring budget and hiring velocity and capture the three main metrics on a hiring scorecard. This scorecard represents the health and impact of the hiring function at your company, and can quickly tell you which components might need some work.

The following visuals, from left to right, are hiring success scorecards for three companies SmartRecruiters has worked with: a North American fast-food restaurant chain with one hundred thousand low-skilled employees; a global manufacturing giant with tens of thousands of engineers and machinery operators; and a Silicon Valley gaming software development company with one thousand employees.

In the first example, the scorecard for the fast-food company shows an amazing hiring velocity of 90 percent. But their hiring budget was 5 percent of salary, on the low side. And their average candidate quality rating or net hiring score was a dreadful -20. Clearly, this organization was investing little in hiring and quickly placing the wrong people on the job. And they paid for this careless approach with high turnover, poor performers, and low team performance. Once they automated their process so they wouldn't lose their hiring velocity, everything turned around. In six months, the fast-food chain had bumped their net hiring score closer to 0, the midpoint.

The second scorecard, for the global manufacturing giant, shows a positive hiring score of 5, a hiring budget of 8 percent, and a good hiring velocity of 70 percent. To improve their

NHS, the company raised their hiring budget from a perfectly respectable 8 percent to a more aggressive 12 percent. As a result, the manufacturing giant's net hiring score went up to 11 while maintaining their existing hiring velocity. The hiring scorecard successfully convinced the company to start managing their recruiting process like a business function, rather than a cost center.

Finally, we have the gaming software company, with a net hiring score of 35. They were hiring amazing talent and spending generously on their hiring budget—12 percent of payroll. They also had a robust recruiting team, but they were sourcing all candidates directly, which slowed their hiring velocity to just 40 percent—meaning only 40 percent of positions were filled on time. Once the company understood that cherry picking every candidate was expensive, slow, and not a scalable way to grow, they changed their sourcing strategy. The new approach was to build a pipeline to attract and nurture larger volumes of candidates. This brought more efficiency to their job funnel, increasing velocity to 65 percent.

Armed with your hiring scorecard, you too will set clear goals for your company's future—and ensure meaningful hiring success.

KEY TAKEAWAYS

- Faster, cheaper metrics like time-to-fill and cost-per-hire are not a measure of hiring success.

- Achieving hiring success means measuring your hiring goals through a hiring budget, hiring velocity, and net hiring score (NHS).

- Hiring budget is the cost of recruiting as a percentage of the total salary of new hires. It measures your level of investment in recruiting as it relates to the market value of new hires (salary), akin to customer acquisition cost ratio.

- Hiring velocity is the percentage of jobs filled on time. It correlates to business velocity by measuring your ability to hire desired skillsets in the time frame necessary to meet business objectives.

- Net hiring score is a strategic hiring success metric that informs recruiting performance in a timely manner and helps to drive hiring strategy. It measures the fit between new hires and jobs.

LET'S GET CANDIDATES

CHAPTER 5

YOU NEED
A STRATEGY

"Geez! It's so hard to find good candidates." I hear this frequently from business leaders and recruiters, but it's not true. Imagine your chief marketing officer (CMO) saying, "Geez! It's so hard to find customers." How would you react? I promise, the candidates are out there, so either you have a poor product—meaning your company brand, roles, and pay are the problem—or, more likely, you're not thinking about candidate attraction as a marketing challenge.

Acquiring candidates is as simple, or complex, as acquiring customers. The good news: you already know how to attract customers, which means you also know how to acquire candidates. As with marketing products for sale, hiring today is about segmentation, conversions, channels, customer acquisition costs, and, most of all, it's about ruthless optimization. Of course, there's definitely art and creativity involved, but for better or worse, hiring has become a high-tech function where data rules.

THE TWO BIGGEST CHALLENGES FACING RECRUITERS TODAY

I. PEOPLE

Traditional recruiters are not data-driven marketers; they like people, not dashboards. But in the data-driven world of competitive hiring, recruiters need to adapt and reinvent themselves to the core. This transition has proven difficult. When you shift your hiring model from traditional recruiting to a sales and marketing function, you need to ask yourself, *Am I putting talented marketers in charge, or asking my recruiters to become marketers?*

2. TECHNOLOGY

Just as modern marketers have embraced digital marketing software systems, so must recruiters adapt to the digital age. Unfortunately, all too many recruiters are stuck in the dark ages, using twenty-year-old applicant tracking systems. Even worse, their systems are often folded into their companies' human resource information systems (HRIS)—lumped with payroll and record keeping. This is like asking a CMO to use an accounting system as their marketing software to save money. It doesn't make any sense!

We will talk more about how to leverage people, technology, and processes to scale hiring success in part 3.

So, yes, your organization is struggling to "find great candidates," but not because it's hard. Rather, you're likely struggling because you're not resourced properly and not invested in the right tech stack.

SEGMENTING YOUR TARGET MARKET

Let's change our thinking and look at candidates as customers for a moment. Imagine you're in the business of selling jobs to the best, most productive talent. So how would your CMO approach the challenge? Chances are she'd start by understanding her target customers and segmenting them. In order to get the clearest picture possible of this target candidate, the CMO would ask herself the following questions:

1. How important and impactful is this person's role to the business?

2. How hard is it going to be to find such a person— i.e., how scarce is this person's specific talent?

Using these two dimensions of value and scarcity, we can now segment talent into one of the following categories.

THE FOUR MAIN CATEGORIES OF TALENT

1. **High scarcity, high impact (Unicorns):** Unicorns are expensive to locate, because they are in scarce supply, and desperately valuable to the business. Some examples include lead executives, neurosurgeons, professors, star traders, and the head of production. The ultimate Unicorn: the CEO.

2. **High scarcity, low impact (Specialists):** Specialists have a lower impact than Unicorns, but they are in short supply and, therefore, challenging to find. These types of roles include nurses, software developers, and truck drivers. Their specialized skills make them hard to find, but their low-to-medium impact makes it unrealistic to generously invest in sourcing them.

3. **Low scarcity, high impact (Professionals):** Professionals are easy to find, but they will have a high impact on your organization, so quality is extremely important. These roles include midlevel managers, marketers, salespeople, and consultants.

4. **Low scarcity, low impact (Core):** Your Core staffers are easy to find and have limited individual impact on the business. These would be your back-office, administrative, and support roles.

Which marketing channels are most effective for attracting candidates? Let's take a look.

TALENT ATTRACTION CHANNELS

For simplicity, we'll divide the multitude of marketing strategies into five main buckets: advertising, content marketing, direct sourcing, referrals, and internal mobility.

ADVERTISING

Say you're a company selling new bed linens: what's the plan? Promote your product and attract attention with media— TV, social, radio, and the internet—right? The same rules apply to recruiting for low-scarcity roles, including Cores and Professionals. These jobs should be advertised on boards like Monster, CareerBuilder, StepStone, LinkedIn, and Seek. Search engines and social media platforms should also be leveraged. You can even hang a "We're Hiring" sign on your storefront. These are the easiest and cheapest forms of candidate attraction, well suited for low-scarcity segments.

CONTENT MARKETING

Content marketing is a method of attracting and nurturing potential customers over time through methods like white papers, webinars, and events. Ultimately, the goal is to convert those engaged prospects into active customers. This method can be applied to recruiting as well. You can create content that attracts and engages potential candidates, nurturing them until you are ready to hire. This sophisticated and effective form of candidate attraction optimizes both the quantity and quality of your recruiting pipeline. Content marketing is ideal for Specialists and can be leveraged for Professionals and Cores as well. It's less effective for those few-and-far-between Unicorns.

DIRECT SOURCING

Sourcing customers through direct prospecting (phone, email, social media, etc.) is another effective marketing tool for recruiters to adopt. When driven by social media and supported by modern, outbound marketing software such as Outreach, this sells certain products well. (Starbucks isn't cold-calling their customers, but life insurance is often sold this way). Similarly, in recruiting, companies can source and market directly to specific candidates through LinkedIn Recruiter, the modern phonebook. Many companies are investing heavily in this strategy. Why? They've been convinced by savvy marketers that advertising is no longer the best model. Not true. Advertising is absolutely more cost-effective than direct sourcing for most talent segments. Reserve the "smile and dial" approach for Unicorns, and occasionally Specialists, but forget it for Professionals and Cores.

REFERRALS

Word of mouth is a popular and effective form of marketing. When Dropbox launched in 2010, users sent 2.8 million direct referrals, increasing signup by 60 percent. You could fairly say that Facebook acquired its two-billion-plus users through referrals, too. They've never had to run ads to acquire anyone—only to justify their behaviors. In recruiting, employee referrals are a powerful tool for sourcing quality candidates across all segments. But you must apply unique strategies for each segment.

INTERNAL MOBILITY

It's widely accepted by marketers that upselling your existing customers is significantly easier than acquiring new ones. Similarly, promoting current employees is low risk and saves time and money—especially for senior and high-impact positions. Marketing to employees is, therefore, a key channel. At Sodexo, for example, over 50 percent of hires come from the existing talent pool.

BUDGETING FOR YOUR TEAM

Once you've segmented your target markets and identified the funnel tactics that work best for each segment, it's time to build a candidate acquisition strategy and budget. In a nutshell, you'll start with your hiring plan for the year and segment it.

CASE STUDY: SMARTRECRUITERS' 2019 HIRING STRATEGY

At SmartRecruiters, we're scaling fast with 70 percent year-over-year growth. In 2019, we started with 225 people, and our model had us at 310 by the end of the year. After factoring in churn, we plan to hire approximately 100 new people.

How do I budget for that strategy? As the CEO, let's imagine I'm committed to investing 5 percent of new-hire salaries into Candidate Attraction each year. With an average salary of $100,000, and 100 recruits needed to scale and fill churn, I have approximately $500,000 to invest. Obviously, I will disproportionately invest in high-scarcity Unicorns and Specialists and less in low-scarcity Professionals and Cores. A sample budget follows.

SmartRecruiters' 2019 Candidate Attraction Budget

Twenty Unicorns: $280,000

Unicorns for SmartRecruiters include lead executives, senior managers, and enterprise sales representatives. We specifically need senior people who understand HR software and can sell seven-figure contracts to large organizations.

At an average annual salary of $200,000, our new-hire salaries amount to $4 million in spending. Unicorns are in short supply, and critical to our business, so we allocate 7 percent of $4 million—$280,000—to candidate attraction. The bulk of the budget funds outbound marketing—a full-time, senior sourcer to directly identify candidates. Additionally, we reserve enough budget to hire a headhunter once or twice a year, and we still advertise to tap into the active market.

Twenty Specialists: $90,000

These are almost exclusively software developers that we're adding as we scale our research and development (R&D) investments.

With an average salary of $90,000, the total spent on new-hire salaries is $1.8 million. We allocate 5 percent of that for a hiring budget of $90,000. This covers a full-time marketer who runs content marketing campaigns, meetups, and programs to attract developers into our core markets—nurturing candidates over time. We do not allocate any budget for outbound sourcing, but as with Unicorns, we still advertise.

Thirty Professionals: $72,000

Professionals at SmartRecruiters consist of customer success managers, sales engineers, and hiring-success consultants.

The average salary is $80,000, bringing the total in new-hire salaries to $2.4 million. We allocate 3 percent of this figure, $72,000, to recruiting. The majority of the budget, roughly $500,000 per position, goes toward advertising. We use programmatic advertising software to buy digital advertising for optimal returns. Additionally, we directly source roles when needed, which accounts for about 25 percent of the positions.

Thirty Cores: $36,000

Our Cores handle general and administrative (G&A) functions, such as customer support and sales development. These are entry-level workers who grow up with us through the ranks.

These entry-level jobs pay $60,000 on average, making up a total salary pool of $1.8 million. We allocate 2 percent to recruiting Cores, about $36,000—or just over $100 per position. This budget is used almost exclusively to attract organic traffic through Google Jobs, Indeed, and some advertising.

30 Professionals	**20 Unicorns**
Consultants, Customer Success Managers, Sales Engineers, Marketers	*Executives, Enterprise Sales Reps (able to close large 7-figure business deals)*
ADVERTIZING - $72K (3%)	**DIRECT SOURCING - $280K (7%)**
30 Core	**20 Specialists**
Sales Development Representative, General & Administrative roles (e.g., Accountant), Support representative	*Software Developers*
ORGANIC - $36K (2%)	**RECRUITMENT MARKETING / CRM - $90K (5%)**

(Vertical axis: IMPACT; Horizontal axis: SCARCITY)

HOW TO MEASURE RETURNS

Now we have a strategy. We understand our segments and channels. And finally, there's a budget. How do we carefully measure returns? As with marketing expenses, everything can and should be measured. The metrics are pretty much the same as well: it's all about conversions and costs. But before you can measure these things, you need to properly track the source of candidate leads.

Every good marketer will agonize over the source of their customer acquisitions. Recruiting is the same. You must be certain that your organization is tracking it properly through documentation. Track the following:

- **Source of acquisition:** Where did we get this candidate? What's the first source?

- **Source of application:** What event triggered the application? Where did the application come from?

The source of acquisition and the source of application might be different. For example, if the candidate saw the job on LinkedIn, but originally connected with the organization two years earlier through a referral, then the source of acquisition is the referral and the source of application is LinkedIn. Make sense? The source is particularly important when managing large talent pools. It's critical to know how you are acquiring candidates, and how you are converting them into potential employees. Tracking data requires a single candidate record, linked to all of your recruitment and marketing activities. By the way, this is exactly what marketers do in their customer relationship management (CRM) systems—track all of the customers' activities in one place. Recruiters must do this also to understand key metrics.

CANDIDATE TO INTERVIEW RATIO: LESS IS MORE

So, now you've attracted a collection of interested candidates. How many of them are good enough to interview? This metric is a measure of quality. For example, from a headhunter you'd expect a 1:1 ratio—they should only introduce qualified candidates primed to interview. High-traffic job boards, on the other hand, might have a 60:1 ratio. This is problematic because filtering through sixty resumes to find the perfect one is time consuming and increases processing costs.

While the digital job market has made things easier than ever for applicants, many companies now find themselves buried in an exhausting pile of resumes—most from unqualified candidates. Given that taking inbound applications is the fastest way to fill jobs, how do you reconcile this? The key: less is more. Part of the recruiting game is convincing fewer people to apply. You don't want two hundred average candidates. You want the five best. So you should be advertising only to qualified prospects in relevant places. A low candidate-to-interview ratio is your best gauge for ensuring that your marketing strategies are driving high-quality applicants.

CLICK-TO-APPLY RATIO: YOUR BEST BET FOR OPTIMIZING CONVERSIONS

A common complaint among talent acquisition specialists: "If it's too easy to apply, we get too many applicants." Incorrectly, they believe that making the online application process more difficult will drive less serious and desirable candidates away. This is a terrible strategy. Drop-off rates for *all* candidates are directly correlated to the amount of time it takes to apply.

Research shows that if the process takes longer than two minutes, you lose up to *80* percent of your traffic.[14] Who abandons first? I'll tell you: it's the highly talented, busy candidate—precisely the one you didn't want to lose.

The online application process must be seamless. This is an impossibility on outdated applicant tracking systems, which average a conversion rate of 5 percent or less. On mobile devices, the conversion rates plummet to 1.5 percent. Why would you pay to send traffic to a page that drives away at least 95 percent of your prospects? If this happened to your CMO, she would be losing it. And yet, most Fortune 500 companies are still stuck with these outdated systems.

If you're wondering whether mobile is *that* important, the answer is yes. At SmartRecruiters, we process tens of millions of applications annually, and mobile devices represent over half of them.

COST PER INTERVIEWED CANDIDATE

The cost per interviewed candidate measures the cost-effectiveness of each marketing channel. This is even more relevant than the cost per applicant. Imagine Indeed sends you 200 applicants at $5 per applicant. If there are 4 good candidates in

---

14 CareerBuilder 2017 Candidate Experience Report.

this pool, your actual cost is $250 per interviewed candidate. LinkedIn, on the other hand, sends you 100 candidates at $10 per candidate. If there are 10 good candidates in this batch, the actual cost of marketing through LinkedIn is $100 per interviewed candidate. In this hypothetical scenario, that's clearly the better deal.

Now that you're armed with the right strategy and metrics, let's talk advertising.

KEY TAKEAWAYS

- Attracting great candidates is essentially a marketing problem. Start thinking of candidates like customers.

- Segmenting talent by impact and scarcity will help you define the appropriate strategy and budget allocation.

- Your five main marketing channels are advertising, content marketing, outbound, referral, and upsells.

- As with marketing, hiring today is about metrics, conversions, channels, candidate acquisition costs, and, most of all, it's about ruthless optimization.

CHAPTER 6

THE POWER OF ADVERTISING

MEN WANTED for Hazardous Journey. Small wages, bitter cold, long months and complete darkness, constant danger, safe return doubtful. Honor and recognition in case of success.

That's a powerful job advertisement. It has a specific target audience and tells it like it is, which is exactly what Sir Ernest Shackleton intended when hiring a crew for his legendary Imperial Trans-Antarctic Expedition of 1914. And it worked. Shackleton needed a specific candidate pool, and the ad attracted the attention of many eager, brave souls.

This is the holy grail of job advertising—to attract a small quantity of highly qualified candidates, measured by applicant-to-interview ratio and cost-per-interviewed candidate (as discussed in the previous chapter). Done well, advertising should provide more than 60 percent of your company's Core and Professional hires—sometimes even bringing you Specialists and those rare Unicorn employees.

Advertising remains one of the best ways to attract active candidates. And with automated email notifications common in many of today's most well-known and powerful job platforms, sometimes even passive candidates can be tempted to apply. For example, platforms like LinkedIn often email relevant candidates a curated list of relevant job opportunities, resulting in a bounty of potential leads for job advertisers.

Unfortunately, many companies don't do advertising well. I often hear HR professionals complain they believe job advertising is dead and solid candidates no longer apply online; they're buried in irrelevant profiles, and the inbound talent pool has all but dried up, leaving outbound as the only reliable strategy. But the problem isn't job advertising doesn't work; the problem is we haven't been doing job advertising properly. So, how *does it work?*

A JOB AD IS AN AD: IT SHOULD SELL

I hate to break it to you, but you're probably writing bad job ads. First of all, a job ad is an ad; it's not meant to be a job description. Consider Shackleton's mini-opus as an illustration. The ad didn't say, "Men Wanted. Duties will include hoisting sails, dropping anchor, frequent rowing, occasional running from bears." Instead, he wrote precisely to his intended audience—risk-taking men seeking adventure who prized glory above money and safety.

Today, the Shackletons of the world no longer write their own job ads; recruiting is treated as an administrative task rather than a marketing and sales function. Sadly, we've allowed job ads to become full-on detailed lists of duties and qualifications, with very little room for motivational advertising language. The end result amounts to largely boring descriptions that few people actually read. As a result, candidates with TLDR (too long, didn't read) Syndrome have sketchy knowledge at best of what they're applying for, thus diluting your candidate pool and wasting everyone's time. Add to this that more than 50 percent of candidates are reading job ads on their phones, and it's no wonder there's a disconnect.

An efficient and robust job ad should include:

- Clean and concise copy
- Attractive design, with a clear call to action
- A focus on the applicant
- The aspirational outcome for the applicant

When it doubt, remember: it's not about you; it's about the applicant. In a recent study by the University of Vermont, researchers looked at 56 ads to which 991 applicants had replied. The ads were split into two groups; those that focused on what the employer *wanted from* the candidate, and those that focused on what the employer *offered to* the applicant. Sure enough, ads focusing on the *applicants* were three times as likely to get higher-quality candidates.

Now that you know what goes into a great job ad, let's talk about how you can use these key ingredients to your greatest advantage.

WHERE SHOULD YOU ADVERTISE?

In the "old days," job openings were posted on signs at the entrance of a factory or store. With the internet came online job boards like Monster. The online job-listing marketplace today is an enormous industry worth nearly $12.5 billion[15] and dominated by a handful of major players—LinkedIn, Recruit, Glassdoor, Indeed, Seek, and StepStone—who control 50 percent of the game. But they're just the (giant) tip of the iceberg. There are thousands of reputable job boards in the U.S. alone, many on content sites that leverage the listings to monetize their traffic and add value for their existing

---

15 Job Board Market, 2017.

audience—a winning combination. Job boards are so lucrative, in fact, that these days, every website and their brother—from BerlinStartupJobs to the International Society of Pediatric Oncology—sooner or later launches one.

The proliferation of job boards presents a significant challenge for organizations when it comes to choosing the best home for their job ads. Unfortunately, the technology gap between online advertising and online job advertising is wide, about ten years wide. Recruiters don't yet have the luxury of targeting ads to ultra-precise demographics across numerous sites at once. Whereas a marketer for Nike can advertise across multiple platforms to women aged eighteen to twenty-seven with medium-high incomes who like basketball and recently visited the Nike website but abandoned their purchase halfway through, recruiters' options for placing job ads are far more limited.

Still, you do have options when it comes to optimizing your job advertising budget. So, what is the right approach: Stick to what you know because it's what you know? Or spread your recruiting wings?

DON'T WASTE YOUR AD BUDGET ON "SPRAY AND PRAY"

Selecting the right job board can be a daunting task, even for the savviest media expert. So, how about the average recruiter with a sketchy understanding of the media landscape? She's just taking her best shot in the dark. That's why the main media strategy in today's recruiting industry is known as "spray and pray," reaching out and interviewing as many candidates as you can in hopes of eventually finding a good one. This is not an efficient use of your budget. Recruiters are given the task to post jobs, but unfortunately an estimated 30 percent of a company's budget is lost by misallocation or overconsumption.

We need to do better than asking our recruiters to post jobs and hope for good results. Some companies try to compensate by automatically posting jobs and centralizing job postings on a single platform, such as LinkedIn. While this sounds nice and simple, and it actually is, obviously not all jobs are created equal; a single job board will not perform well across all segments, industries, and functions.

THE PROS AND CONS OF PERFORMANCE-BASED ADVERTISING

Driven by job search engines like Indeed and soon Google Jobs, the market is steadily moving toward performance-based advertising. That's the good news. Using Indeed's integrated tools, employers can understand cost per candidate, cost per click, and cost per applicant. This last metric isn't easy to quantify, however, since neither Indeed nor Google track who or how many people apply through their links, let alone who makes it to an interview, receives an offer, or gets hired.

Performance-based job search engines may have become a formidable source of leads for employers, but they pose two challenges. First, they sell volume while you need quality. Receiving two hundred or five hundred or one thousand resumes isn't useful; receiving ten good ones, on the other hand, is very useful. The incentive of volume is simply not the right one for job search engines. Secondly, budget allocation by job is difficult and time consuming. In fact, if you consider each job as a campaign, it's a mammoth task to optimize it all. But it's necessary.

Imagine you have an open job and just received two excellent candidate referrals who are both moving toward the final interview stage. Do you really need to spend more money to attract more new candidates? Obviously not. Ideally, you'd pause your job ad at this stage, but you probably won't, since you're not tracking the process at that level of granularity. And that means a lot of wasted budget.

PROGRAMMATIC JOB ADVERTISING: THE NEW GOLD STANDARD

Ultimately, the job advertising market is moving—along with many segments of online advertising—toward proper programmatic job advertising. Programmatic advertising employs a machine in place of a human to say, "Let me display this ad, to this user, at this moment in time, on this website; because I know this user exhibits this behavior, or I know this website is a relevant one." For example, in the product advertising arena today, a women's basketball athletic-wear marketer doesn't buy a single ad on WNBA.com; she buys traffic across a multitude of sites frequented by women aged eighteen to twenty-seven who like basketball.

Programmatic advertising is still rarely used for recruitment, comprising only 0.1 percent of the total job advertising market. While candidate ads might occasionally pop up on Pinterest, plenty of recruiting sites would rather take your money directly than be part of an advertising network, and, as such, they are resisting the change. For example, programmatic advertising is not currently possible on LinkedIn. A company must purchase a job slot and yearly fee in order to post jobs one at a time. But Google Jobs is coming, and given that 30 percent of all job searches start on Google, it's safe to say that programmatic job advertising is an emerging force, bound to take off as talent acquisition leaders begin to grasp its value.

At SmartRecruiters, for example, we've been developing a product called SmartJobs. It delivers budget optimization by selecting and posting job ads to thousands of websites, including Indeed, LinkedIn, Facebook, Pinterest, and even the preferred candidate's favorite niche blogs. The system constantly re-allocates and optimizes ad spend based on the quality of applicants that are actually coming through the client's door.

Like SmartJobs, any programmatic ad solution meriting your consideration must:

- Understand your recruiting needs
- Know where to best find that traffic
- Optimize your budget with the best possible purchase

This technology is embedded inside your recruitment software suite, so it knows when jobs open and close, when you need more or fewer candidates, who gets interviewed, who gets hired, and from which source. In a nutshell, once you've set some parameters such as budget and maximum time to be spent per type of job (Unicorn, Specialist, Professional, and Core), a programmatic ad solution will optimize everything for you, from job posting through job hire.

OPTIMIZE, OPTIMIZE, OPTIMIZE!

Congratulations! You now know the secret to creating an irresistible job ad and distributing it to the most relevant sites. Alas, none of that matters if you don't optimize for conversions. So, let's look closer at the three layers of conversion optimization:

1. BEFORE APPLY

In this stage, you verify that the job ad was written properly, with a clear call to action. Proof of this is in the pudding, measurable by candidate views-to-apply conversion. Of all the people who viewed the ad, how many clicked on "Apply"? Usually less than 6 percent, per job advertising vendor Appcast.

A well-written ad is requisite for a high percentage of apply clicks. But, even assuming you've created a masterpiece, there are still lots of little things at play. For example, in 2011 we changed the SmartRecruiters "Apply Now" button to a friendlier "I'm Interested," and our average views-to-apply ratio doubled from 10 to 20 percent. At $1 per click, the cost of acquiring 100 applicants used to be $1,000. Now, you'd be spending $500, a 50 percent savings!

2. DURING APPLY

The apply process is the most visible part of any broken recruiting technology platform. When faced with a long, convoluted application form, most people simply don't bother; at least not the kind of candidate you'd like to see.

To illustrate, let's say you want to attract 100 candidates. Applying a 5 percent conversion rate typically seen on a dated recruiting platform versus 30 percent on a modern one like

SmartRecruiters offers, you'll end up paying $2,000 (for 2,000 job ad clicks) versus $333. Factoring in mobile-device trends makes it even worse. Mobile click-throughs make up only about a 1.2 percent conversion, meaning that for every 100 candidates who click through, only one will complete their job application. Can you imagine your CMO sending traffic to a landing page that drops 95 to 99 percent of people who intend to purchase? Be sure to watch your click-to-apply conversion rate and optimize accordingly.

3. AFTER APPLY

In this stage, you measure and optimize the quality of incoming resumes, best accomplished by the applicant-to-interview ratio. As a benchmark, anything under twenty reviewed resumes to find one good one is considered a well-targeted campaign.

LinkedIn delivers an applicant-to-interview ratio of 27:1. We're working on bringing that ratio down, but it still beats Indeed at 44:1, and Craigslist at 68:1—clearly demonstrating candidate quality.

When all's said and done, applying the three layers of optimization conversion is key to fully leveraging your advertising efforts.

PULLING IT ALL TOGETHER

The recipe for good job advertising is precise, yet uncomplicated. First, the job ad should be enticing and designed for both mobile and desktop viewing. Second, it should ensure that your jobs are displayed on the right channel with optimal ad spend; this may mean experimenting with programmatic advertising, managing your campaigns on job search engines on a more granular level, or allocating your job board budget more precisely and with essential management. And last but not least, it's essential to study your conversion metrics and create a plan for optimization.

Shackleton's "hazardous journey with doubtful safe return" may not have ended in a successful land crossing of the Antarctic, but the explorer and all but three members of his intrepid twenty-eight-man team survived a feat of endurance that earned them the "honor and recognition" promised upon return. And all of this was thanks to a well-crafted job ad. Advertising remains the number-one source of hire for businesses around the world, so why not put this powerful medium to work for you?

KEY TAKEAWAYS

- A job ad is an ad, not a job description. Keep ad copy clean and concise, with an attractive design, a clear call to action, and a focus on the applicant.

- Job advertising, like any online advertising, requires proper targeting optimized through a performance-based programmatic solution.

- Programmatic job advertising solutions best allocate spending if they are connected to your recruiting process and tracking which job should go where and when.

- Conversion optimization is particularly critical at the apply stage, where 95 percent drop-off rates are not uncommon.

CHAPTER 7

PRIMING THE
PIPELINE

n early 2019, McDonald's Canada launched a campaign that allowed people to literally apply for a job through Snapchat. Candidates simply loaded a picture of themselves into a McDonald's filter, cleverly called a Snapplication. The campaign went viral, and McDonald's received nearly ten thousand Snapplications in forty-eight hours—enough to refill the talent pipeline for 1,200 Canadian stores.

This example is a vivid testament to modern digital marketing's power to attract talent. And it's replicable if your organization approaches the challenge from a marketing perspective rather than a traditional talent acquisition perspective. What does that mean?

PIPELINING LIKE A MARKETER

Let's imagine you're a large Fortune 50 company working hard at designing self-driving cars, and you need to acquire one hundred data scientists for your new office in the heart of Silicon Valley. Competition is fierce.

If your recruiting organization approaches the search using old-school TA techniques, here's what's probably going to happen: they will leverage LinkedIn and start cold-calling. When this proves to be a struggle, they'll resort to using headhunters, who'll charge 20 percent on the salary of each candidate placed. Before you know it, your hiring budget has exploded and your net hiring score is negative because you've compromised on B-players.

Now let's tackle that search as a marketer would approach a customer attraction campaign. In other words, your talent acquisition team will divide the search into four main stages: *acquire, qualify, nurture, convert.*

ACQUIRE

To attract the best candidates, you might start with an offer, a white paper, an event, or a meetup that appeals to the talent pool you're after.

In our hypothetical search for one hundred data scientists, you might start by asking your chief scientist to write a white paper on the challenges of data modeling for self-driving cars. The logic here: anyone interested in the data-modeling challenges for self-driving cars is likely a data scientist or at the very least highly motivated to learn to be, with skills to match.

Your TA team will upload the paper to a nicely designed landing page and drive traffic to it through social networks. Maybe they'll add a $1,000 advertising budget for a handful of Google Ad words or a display ad for people interested in this topic. Once a few weeks have passed, let's say one thousand leads will have accessed your download. (For reference, one thousand is a low estimate; any solid content should bring in tens of thousands of hits.)

QUALIFY

As part of the online lead capture form, your TA team will have started the qualification process by building a few simple "check the box" questions like "Which of the following data-science technologies have you used in the past?" into the white paper download box. The questions will have been carefully chosen because each will have an impact on conversion. The team now leverages the candidates' answers to focus on those who have the right skillset for a data scientist job. Now, you're down to eight hundred "interesting" or "qualified" candidates.

NURTURE

It's time to get your eight hundred leads to a point where they're interested in exploring career opportunities with your company. Your team will set up a simple email drip campaign so that all eight hundred prospects who downloaded the white paper are invited to a follow-up webinar hosted by your chief scientists. Those who join the webinar might subsequently be invited to a meetup at your office for a panel debate on dataset trends for self-driving cars. After this step, about four hundred people will have attended the webinar or the meetup or both and have a growing interest in your company. Excellent; now it's time to make things happen.

CONVERT

At this point you can start marketing jobs to the four hundred people engaged with your company. Have your team send out a simple email: "We're hiring. Would you be interested in talking to us?" They'll follow that up with personal-touch emails and direct approaches. Statistically speaking, about half of those candidates will be interested in chatting. Those two hundred candidates will be routed to a recruiter for phone screening, then a round of interviews onsite.

Fast-forward four weeks. You've spent $1,000 on the ad campaign and bought a lot of pizzas for the team. The campaign has been managed by a junior marketer, with contributions from your chief scientist, who will do most anything to hire great people because she understands that you are who you hire. Now your recruiting team is fishing in an active pipeline barrel of more than two hundred top data scientists who understand what you are trying to achieve and want to be part of it.

Recruiting problem solved. Your hiring velocity for the year will be 100 percent and your net hiring score will be 30 because now you can afford to be picky. In addition, your hiring budget will be under 1 percent, which is a fraction of the more than $1 million that companies would normally spend to hire one hundred data scientists. Job well done.

If it's that easy, you might be wondering, why aren't more companies doing it?

Some companies are. Take Atlassian, an Australian software company that made headlines with their European "We're Coming for Your Geeks" campaign. The company did a bus tour through four European cities to hire fifteen developers in fifteen days. The campaign went viral, and they received far more applications than they ever imagined. They did it again in 2015 for designers with the tagline, "We're seeking design thinkers, talented thinkers, and wannabe surfers to join us in the sunshine of Australia." Atlassian staff climbed into a company-branded Volkswagen van with a surfboard and toured multiple cities in Europe: London, Amsterdam, Berlin, and Stockholm. Once again, they scored big.

For most organizations, however, leveraging digital marketing for talent attraction at scale remains an opportunity more than a reality. And the barriers are the same as usual: people and technology.

JUMP THE BARRIERS TO PIPELINE-BUILDING SUCCESS

There's no way around it: you need an experienced marketer on your recruiting team. A recruiter or sourcer can learn to be a marketer, but it's actually a completely different skillset and mindset. The former is all about candidates, skills, and deadlines, while the latter understands segments, conversions, automation, and volume. If you want to leverage digital marketing as a source of candidates, hire a marketer and give them the task of creating a pipeline for your desired talent type.

Your new recruiting marketer will need some basic tools, such as design and web development, but you already have all of that within your marketing team. They will also require good technology to create landing pages, signup forms, qualification criteria, email campaigns, and drip campaigns. Unfortunately, most recruiting teams don't have access to this technology, as they're usually forced to work on old applicant tracking systems. These are generally stand-alone systems that make it impossible to keep a unified candidate record. Without proper software, your recruiting marketer may end up marketing jobs to someone you actually rejected last week. That reflects badly on you and has the potential to cause all kinds of in-house snags.

The solution to all of this is a dedicated talent acquisition suite that covers the full set of marketing functionality and ATS in one setting, allowing you to maintain every candidate's record. Applying digital marketing techniques to your TA suite can be totally transformative, especially for your expert segments, where candidates are hard to find but you need lots of them. Think like McDonald's: ready, set, snap.

KEY TAKEAWAYS

- Modern digital marketing is a powerful channel to attract large volumes of talent in a very cost-effective way.

- Candidate attraction campaigns should be structured like a marketing funnel—from acquire to qualify to nurture to convert.

- Pipelining is a critical yet often overlooked part of any good talent attraction strategy.

- A single marketing campaign can outperform a large team of recruiters or sourcers.

CHAPTER 8

FINDING THE NEEDLE
IN A HAYSTACK

ack in 2001, Larry Page and Sergei Brin set out to find a CEO for Google, their then young startup company. They scratched off about fifty powerful Silicon Valley execs and turned to Eric Schmidt, who at the time was running the multibillion-dollar software company Novell. Before making Schmidt an offer, Page and Brin did something unusual; they brought him to Burning Man. For the uninitiated, Burning Man is effectively a utopian gathering where cash is forbidden and monetary transactions are not allowed. Ironically, one of the most significant hires in history happened at a festival known for its anti-capitalist ethos: by the end of the excursion, Google had their Unicorn, and today, Eric Schmidt's reported net worth is nearly $14 billion.

DRAW YOUR UNICORN

When it comes to Unicorn hunting, direct sourcing is the ideal approach. You'll start by painting clear targets. Draw your Unicorn, if you will. In the case of Larry and Sergei, they knew they had to find someone who had scaled and managed a multibillion-dollar software firm and could take Google to the next level. That profile was pretty clear, with a relatively short list of individuals suitable for the role.

The more precise the target, the easier it becomes to identify, contact, and ultimately sell to them. Imagine being given a phone book and being told, "Find me a chief data scientist." Where would you start? On the other hand, if the mandate is narrowed to, "Find me a chief data scientist who has worked in matching jobs to candidates and understands resume data-sets," suddenly the list is a lot shorter and easier to manage.

DIG DEEP

With a clear job profile in hand, you can now dig deep. Really deep. Always start a Unicorn hunt with a direct sourcing target list. When it comes to meeting the criteria we've set, there are probably no more than forty companies who've tried to solve that particular problem—from the brilliant crew at LinkedIn to job boards like ZipRecruiter and Stepstone to startups like Entelo or Clustree. Your team will begin preparing a list of all individuals to target. To nail this market research, you need a researcher, or sourcer, as they are most commonly called in recruiting. Someone who will call dozens of people to understand the market and track down names and references of qualified potential candidates.

The question they ask is simple: "Who is the best chief scientist in recruiting tech?" There's no point in contacting all forty or even twenty-five of the candidates your resource brings you; what you really want to know is, who are the *best* ones? Build that list and then start contacting them.

GET INVOLVED

Most execs will just sit back and wait for interested candidates to show up for interviews. That's a big mistake. Similar to Larry and Sergei, you have to get involved because *you* are selling, not your sourcer or recruiter. A senior headhunter might be able to kick-start a conversation and a process for you, but ultimately the job of selling is yours.

If you're going Unicorn hunting, that's what it takes.

Assuming your sourcer has done a great job qualifying people, you should be able to narrow the list to a handful of names, write the emails, and make the calls. Top talent gets calls every week, so you need to do everything in your power to intrigue these highly sought-after candidates.

I speak from experience, having used this technique to hire a general manager for SmartRecruiters in London. I built a list of the best recruiting software sales leaders in the UK, narrowed it down, and cross-referenced it. The indicators were very clear: the number-one person for the job was Rob Symons, a director of strategic accounts at a competitive company. I cold-called him and eventually convinced him to come work for us. Within one year, Rob and the great team he assembled brought dozens of strategic, new customers to SmartRecruiters, including giants like Bosch and IKEA. Would he have taken that critical cold call from a junior sourcer? Hard to tell, but in the end it was well worth my time to reach out personally.

RAISE THE BAR

Let's take a look at your Unicorn hunting approach, as it is right now. How high is your bar? Are you hiring the best you can find, or the best in the market? Assuming you're casting a wide-enough net with your job advertising, you have a good evaluation process, and you're making competitive offers, you're likely hiring the best you can find.

But with deep research, a precise job profile, direct sourcing, and a strong sales approach, you can raise that bar. Don't settle for the very best candidate *on* the market when you can have the very best *in* the market—the very best, period.

I learned that nuance as a young headhunter, searching for a senior sales executive for the banking vertical for Cisco Systems in Poland. It was a very precise profile to say the least. I did my research, found three good candidates, and introduced them to my client. After the interviews, the client called back, congratulated me, and said he liked all three. I patted myself on the back, thinking, *Great job: everyone's happy; I can close the search.* Not so fast. The client had an important question: "Jerome, do you think we could find a better one?" Instead of simply hiring one of the three excellent candidates I'd sent him, he sent me back to research to prove that I had left no stone unturned. A wise directive. After redoubling my efforts to reach out to every candidate in the market, we actually did find a superior hire.

WHEN (AND HOW) TO RETAIN A PRO

Keep in mind that deep research and leaving no stone unturned requires a fairly intense investment. If you plan to use an external agency to do this work, then retain them. But avoid the "success-only" payment model. While a "no cure, no pay" deal may sound attractive, it is in fact counterproductive when it comes to Unicorns. An agency working on a success-only basis has no guarantee of making any money, so why would they do any research at all? You may well end up paying high fees to hire the best active person on that agency's roster—not exactly the best candidate on the market, let alone the best in the market.

Paying agencies on a "success-only" basis to find Specialists and Professionals may be an indicator of a deeper problem— your own inability to source candidates. My advice is to limit the use of agencies to Unicorn hunting, and when you do use them, don't be afraid to demand exhaustive research. "Can we find a better one?" is always an excellent question to ask.

WHEN DIRECT SOURCING IS A "DON'T"

When Reid Hoffman founded LinkedIn in 2002, his primary goal was to help connect Professionals. Little did he know that recruiting would become his golden goose, eventually generating nearly $6.8 billion in yearly revenue for his company.[16]

With LinkedIn Recruiter, a sourcer can pay to get access to three hundred million profiles. And with InMail, users can also pay to reach out to specific individuals. With that level

---

16   LinkedIn Economic Graph, 2014.

of efficiency, LinkedIn has made direct sourcing an extremely popular method for recruiters on the hunt not just for Unicorns, but for Specialists and Professionals, too.

I do have some concerns about direct sourcing becoming the default channel for large-scale hiring. In addition to the high cost of direct sourcing candidates at scale, there's the issue of predictability. When you're hunting for needles in the same haystack as all of your competitors, success or failure comes down to luck. You can't predict luck. No wonder the typical velocity for teams that focus purely on direct sourcing for Specialists and Professionals is usually under the acceptable benchmark of 80 percent. Then there's the question: can you really hire the best candidate possible when you have ten searches going on at once? Chances are, you'll compromise, leading to a low overall net hiring score.

The bottom line: once you scale direct sourcing beyond Unicorns into Specialists and Professionals, you'll start to see diminishing returns. Measure the outcomes carefully to know where to draw the line and consider investing in other channels, such as creating a marketing team for pipeline recruiting or revising your existing job advertising strategy for optimal conversion.

Back to those rare Unicorns: once you have one in sight, get involved. With dedicated persistence, you can land the perfect candidate without going to Burning Man.

KEY TAKEAWAYS

- Direct sourcing works best for categories with highly specific skillsets, like Unicorns and some Specialists. It does not scale for large-volume hires (which are best supported by marketing).

- Direct sourcing requires the personal involvement of the hiring manager and offers an opportunity to set the candidate bar high.

- If you use an agency, avoid the "success only" model. Instead, pay a retainer to ensure that they do extensive outreach. And be demanding.

CHAPTER 9

FRIENDS OF MY FRIENDS ARE...

On average, each human is connected to about 500 other people. In the corporate world, if you have 1,000 employees, that's a 500,000-person network. Go two degrees out and you're at 25 million, plus or minus a million or two of overlap. Many of these people likely went to similar schools, worked in similar industries, and are previous colleagues, customers, or partners of your target employee. The truth is, your organization is likely already connected to every single candidate you'll hire next year.

This is good news for you. Research shows that referred workers in all four segments—Cores, Professionals, Specialists, and Unicorns—are a better culture fit at their companies, are 30 percent less likely to quit, and show substantially better performance on high-impact metrics.[17] It's no wonder that employee referral programs are so popular at modern companies like Salesforce, where they account for 53 percent of hires.

The question is, how do you leverage the referral channel to its full potential? Let's start by defining what constitutes a true referral, as this definition can differ greatly between companies.

DEGREES OF REFERRALS

INTRODUCTIONS

An introduction is when a recruiter asks an employee at her company to connect her with an acquaintance or distant cousin. That's all it is, an introduction—not a true referral. The employee is not vouching for the person or the company.

RECOMMENDATIONS

A recommendation is when a recruiter asks a current employee at his company for feedback on a candidate whom the employee has previously worked with. In a reverse scenario, if a candidate is applying to a company where their friend works, they may ask the friend if they recommend working there. Like an

---

17   Ernst & Young, 2016.

introduction, this is not a true referral. No one's actually refer-ring anyone; they're just providing insight.

TRUE REFERRALS

A true referral is a combination of both introduction and rec-ommendation. You know someone who would be great for the role, and you make an introduction and recommendation at the same time. Perhaps you tell your friend Suzie, "You should come work here; this is a good company." To your company, you say, "We should hire Suzie; she's great." That is a proper referral.

WHY YOU SHOULDN'T PAY FOR REFERRALS

Employee referrals can be risky business. What if they get it wrong? What if the friend doesn't perform, or the job doesn't satisfy them? Understandably, employees may be reluctant to put forward candidates for open roles at your company.

Which brings up a good question: are cash incentives the right way to encourage referrals? Experiments have proven that they are not. Google tried doubling referral bonuses from $2,000 to $4,000 and saw very little impact on the actual refer-ral outcomes. In another example, a tech CEO I know in San Francisco decided to offer a $20,000 bonus for senior software developer referrals. Candidate volume went way up, but quality went down because employees were referring anyone and their uncle in hopes of getting that bonus. In the end, the program escalated into an altercation between two of his employees. One of them had referred the other, who took the job when the original employee (disingenuously, it turned out) agreed to split the bounty. When the duo's attempt to game the system came to light, the CEO realized his referral strategy had backfired.

If you want participation, then *reward* participation—don't try to buy it. For example, Salesforce provides two tickets to a San Francisco Giants game for those who make successful referrals, those that make it to the interview stage. I like that a lot. It encourages people to take the risk of submitting a referral but doesn't tempt them to get greedy. A good reward is something that has an impact—a public recognition, a restaurant voucher, a donation to a charity of their choosing, or any of the tactics I list below in "Reward Time" make excellent choices. Just avoid the cash.

Also keep in mind that managers shouldn't be eligible for referral incentives within their teams, but it's interesting to track who they are actually bringing in.

HEALTHY REFERRALS, HEALTHY CULTURE

People want to participate in the success of their company. They want to know their opinion matters. Indeed, most people truly want to make an impact; helping the company or a friend, doing what's right, is what motivates them. A recent LinkedIn survey asked why people referred friends, and the results said it all: 35 percent said they were motivated to help their friends, 30 percent said they wanted to help their company, and 26 percent said they wished to be seen as a valuable colleague. Only 6 percent said they were doing it for money or recognition.

The fact is, employee referrals are solid indicators of your company culture. A good person won't refer their friend to a company they don't like. On the other hand, if someone feels great about a particular company, they will be glad to refer. To illustrate, we can look at the Employee Net Promoters Score (eNPS). This system is widely used to measure employee satisfaction and propensity to refer. The system asks, "How likely are you, on a scale of one to ten, to refer a friend to work here?" An answer of one to five, or not very likely, is an immediate red flag. It generally means the employee simply doesn't like the company. In that regard, a high-performing referral program is a reliable indicator of a healthy company culture and high employee satisfaction.

A solid referral program also socially commits employees to the organization. If someone tells a friend they should come work for a company, the referring person enhances their emotional commitment to the company, reinforcing the fact that referrals are not only a good source of hires but an excellent employee engagement vehicle.

GET THE BASICS RIGHT

To design a good referral program, start with the basics. Employees generally echo the same thoughts in this regard: "If you want me to refer someone, then tell me what jobs are available, make it easy to refer, treat my friend well, and please tell me what happened." It's amazing how few companies actually meet these basic requirements.

On the job side, give your employees a good view of what jobs are available, through a regular sharing of new jobs. Many of your employees know the same people, so focus on jobs within their team or at least their function. For example, send an email to the finance team announcing all current open finance roles. And make it easy; employees should be able to make a referral in just a few clicks. If it's too much hassle, they won't do it. It can be as simple as entering a friend's name and email, and encouraging some context, such as how they know this person. This gives you the opportunity to note that that particular job has a recommendation attached to it; the candidate is not just a friend of a friend who the employee has never met. Ideally, you'd like to see something along the lines of, "We worked together and Suzie's amazing."

It's also good practice to give well-referred candidates the royal treatment. For example, a referred candidate with a recommendation automatically gets a phone screening within forty-eight hours, most likely followed by an interview. On the other hand, a simple introduction with no recommendation need not merit special treatment. This is an excellent way to encourage quality referrals.

Once an employee has made a referral, the candidate (their friend) will naturally turn to them with questions about next steps. Empower all parties by providing transparency at all stages, from "in review," when the candidate's resume is being considered, to "interview" to "offer," to "hired."

REWARD TIME

Once you have the basics of your referral program dialed in, then you can think of it as a marketing program, leveraging creative ideas to encourage quality and volume of referrals.

I take great pleasure in recognizing, even celebrating, any employee who brings a quality referral to SmartRecruiters. I used to reward successful referrals with a weekend getaway for two, on one condition: the employee had to send our office a postcard from the trip. Eventually, we had a wall of postcards sent from magical locations, and it worked like a charm. Every day, people walked by the postcard wall and wondered who they could refer to get their own postcard up there. Let's take a look at some similar referral inspiration programs:

- **Coding:** GoDaddy internally advertised its referral program in code to inspire in-house developers to refer other developers. The strategy nearly doubled their referral output.

- **Competitions:** At Rent-A-Car, employees compete by region to bring in the most referrals. By fostering camaraderie and, sure, offering a generous prize for the winners, the company has managed to acquire a full third of its staff via referrals.

- **Food:** Booking.com was having a hard time finding Portuguese- and English-speaking customer reps for their Brazil operations. When a creative recruiter bought Portuguese food for the entire office and left a note reminding the employees of this shortage, there was a dramatic spike in referrals.

- **Charity:** At Accenture, employees can donate a part of their referral bonus to a preferred charity, and the company matches the amount. This feel-good reward led to a spike in referrals.

- **Gamification:** Fiverr has transparently gamified their employee referral program. Employees are awarded points for job shares on social media, and candidate referrals and statuses are shown on a company leaderboard. Making a game of it boosted their referral numbers.

MEASURING REFERRAL PROGRAMS

If your referrals are genuine recommendations, you should get pretty close to a 1:1 candidate to interview ratio—drastically better than the 60:1 that we see with generic advertising. Keep in mind that on the cost side, a fully loaded referral program should not exceed 3 to 4 percent of new hire salary, making it a very cost-effective source of hire, especially for Specialists and Unicorns.

There's no question that referred hires make excellent hires. So, what are you waiting for? You're already connected to twenty-five million of them.

KEY TAKEAWAYS

- Referred hires outperform their peers across all four segments—Cores, Professionals, Specialists, and Unicorns.

- A proper referral combines an introduction and a recommendation. Do not reward introductions alone.

- Give referred candidates a high degree of attention, and keep referrers informed at all stages.

- Paying for referrals is not the best strategy. Create an incentive program, but match it to your needs and company culture.

CHAPTER 10

HUNT IN YOUR OWN BACKYARD

U p until the 1970s, corporations filled roughly 90 percent of their jobs through promotions and internal hires. In today's fluid marketplace, internal mobility represents only about a third of all hires.[18] Why? Companies mistakenly believe that it's easier and cheaper to lure talent from competitors than to train and develop from within. On the contrary, hiring internally is faster, easier, cheaper, and better for employee engagement and company culture. Let's unpack why.

---

18 Harvard Business Review, 2019.

THE PROS OF INTERNAL HIRING

LOWER RISK

Companies hiring internally are 32 percent more likely to be satisfied with the quality of their new hires.[19] When a candidate's work habits and track record are known and understood, the company is betting on a proven quality, not a wild card.

LOWER COSTS AND FASTER RESULTS

Hiring and training expenses are tremendously reduced when employees are hired from within. It makes sense: internal hires are familiar with company culture, workflows, and policies, which leads to faster engagement and productivity. In addition, it takes about two years for an external hire to reach the same level of performance as an internal hire.[20]

FEWER SILOS

As in the natural world, cross-pollinating within an organization is highly beneficial. When employees change departments, divisions, functions, or even countries, the benefits are numerous: knowledge is shared, communication across

---

19 Deloitte, 2018.
20 Deloitte, 2018.

the organization improves, the skill base gets wider, and silos are removed.

REDUCED EMPLOYEE TURNOVER

Employee turnover is something every CEO cares about, and for good reason. A staggering 83 percent of employees surveyed in 2018 said they wanted a new job.[21] Companies must satisfy that demand by boosting internal mobility, or bear significant expense. Deloitte estimates that a company with thirty thousand employees loses more than $400 million to employee turnover yearly. In total, that churn costs businesses in the United States alone $160 billion a year.[22] By providing employees with the opportunity to find new jobs internally, you'll dramatically reduce your turnover losses while benefiting from an engaged, satisfied team.

EASE OF HIRING FOR OTHER POSITIONS

High-volume, low-scarcity positions are the easiest and cheapest to fill. When you promote from within, people climb the ladder and fill hard-to-find positions. As a result, the majority of jobs you'll need to fill externally are from the easier-to-find Core segment. Imagine you need ten software developers in the

---

21 Harris Interactive, 2018.
22 HR Digest, 2018.

Specialist segment. You fill these roles with ten Core-level soft-ware developers who are replaced by ten interns. Just like that, your software developer hiring challenge has disappeared. Many companies are built on this model. For example, McDonald's never hires managers for their restaurants. Ninety-six percent of their managers started with the company flipping burgers.

WHY COMPANIES STRUGGLE TO HIRE FROM WITHIN

Today's employees, millennials especially, expect the opportu-nity to grow within their organizations. And an overwhelming 94 percent wish their companies would invest more in their careers.[23] So why is it that the majority of workers find it diffi-cult to advance from within?

Two factors contribute to this trend. First, employees are often passive about managing their careers. Traditionally, promo-tions are driven by learning and development; an employee develops necessary skills and is promoted as a result. But while some of those new skills are gained through on-the-job expe-rience, others can only be acquired through training programs and insider opportunities bestowed by managers. This system leaves employees feeling disempowered to take charge of their own growth.

---

23   LinkedIn, 2018.

Second, archaic rules often dictate who is allowed to move through the ranks and how. For example, I once worked with a large bank that required employees to obtain approval from their manager prior to applying for a different internal job. For obvious reasons, the vast majority of employees didn't feel comfortable doing that; instead, they quietly applied at competing financial institutions.

In addition to the retention problem this created, it also encouraged the development of silos and manager chiefdoms that would not let the best talent evolve. Team leaders who were rewarded for producing results but not for promoting internal mobility certainly didn't want to lose high-performing team members. To that end, they created obstacles to mobility for their best workers—finding subtle ways to discourage and even prevent them from moving departments.

While corporate managers are often blamed for blocking internal mobility, I believe the problem starts with the company culture. Nearly half of managers surveyed say they have few, if any, tools to identify and move people into internal roles. And many HR leaders say they believe their companies lack the systems to enable and promote internal hires.[24]

I highly encourage you to take the first step of making it easy for employees to apply anywhere within your company. It's

---

24 Deloitte, 2018.

simply the most efficacious way to circumvent the loss of coveted talent.

REMOVE BARRIERS, REDUCE FRICTION

If you want to solve internal mobility issues, the answer is simple: remove the barriers. For years, managers at Visa conducted their annual reviews and made decisions on promotions at a set time each year. This created a culture with little employee movement in the months leading up to annual reviews. When the new CEO, Al Kelly, arrived in 2016, he noticed that internal mobility rates were low and declared two corporate initiatives to drive change. First, any employee would be encouraged to apply to any internal job at any point in time. Second, a new hub, Visa University, would allow employees to continue learning and upskilling in any field of interest. Within ninety days, this empowered employees to step up to apply, and the rate of internal hires increased significantly. Al also held other senior executives accountable by adding performance metrics around internal mobility, incentivizing managers to proactively collaborate and create internal career paths.

Employees thrive when they are given the power to take charge of their mobility rather than waiting for their managers or HR departments to hand opportunities to them. You can promote this independence by ensuring that new job openings at your organization are transparently posted to your company website. Existing team members should then be able to seamlessly set preferences and apply.

If you wish to implement guidelines around the process, it's best to keep them simple:

- **Who can apply?** Personally, I think anyone should be able to apply for any job at any time, but if that is too much for your organization, a good rule of thumb is that an employee should have a minimum of eighteen months in their job before being free to apply elsewhere in the company.

- **What's the process?** The process should be clear and transparent. While managers should never be given the power to decide if their employees can apply to move internally, they should be informed at least as soon as their team member is interviewing with another department. And most definitely before an offer is made. The rest of the process looks like a simplified version of what is used for external applicants. For example, no background checks are required for in-house employees.

- **What are the implications?** It's critical to ensure that employees know they will be treated well. One global consumer goods company struggling with their company culture set a new expectation that recruiters would have a maximum of forty-eight hours to respond to internal applicants and seventy-two hours to conduct an initial screening, even if the applicant was not quite suited for the role. This tactic made employees feel more connected and engaged with hiring teams and more likely to continue applying for posted roles. The organization's initial target was to fill 10 percent of all open positions with internal candidates, but they went well over that mark, sourcing 30 percent of jobs internally within one year.

LET COMPANY LEADERS DRIVE ENGAGEMENT

Home Depot's company leaders play a key role in driving internal mobility efforts. The company encourages leaders and managers to share their own career trajectories with recent hires. This encourages associates to plan for lateral or vertical career growth inside the company. Importantly, company leaders and managers are rated on their ability to fill talent pipelines with internal candidates, inspiring participation on both the supply and the demand side.

DON'T LET YOUR COMPETITORS BEAT YOU AT EMPLOYEE MARKETING

Your employees are targeted by recruiters every day. If you don't market to your own team, your competitors will not hesitate to take advantage. The war for talent is on, and if you aren't giving employees enticing options and opportunities within your company, watch out. Statistics show that more than half of your current employees would be keen to leave their current job for something better if it came along, and more than 70 percent are already thinking about their next move.[25]

With that kind of data in hand, it's worth making an extra effort to increase internal mobility. I recently learned this lesson at SmartRecruiters. We had a very stable and high-performing team in our engineering department, made up of six engineers who had collectively built many great functionalities together. Over a four-year period, I frequently offered the engineers opportunities to switch teams in order to learn about other aspects of our product—but they really liked working together, so I never pushed the issue. Alas, this past spring a top engineer from the team left because she'd gotten bored. "I wish you'd forced me out of my comfort zone," she told me.

---

25   Randstad, 2018.

Who knows? Maybe things would have gone differently if I'd taken a page from Spotify's playbook. There, employees often have close-ended missions, and they are strongly encouraged to change things up after two years in a role. According to CEO Daniel Ek, this strategy has served his restless, millennial-powered workforce well.[26]

THE FUTURE OF MOBILITY

Is it likely that your company will ever fill 90 percent of jobs internally? Probably not, but you should at least be aiming to fill about half your seats from within. For inspiration, just look to Sodexo, where half of all hiring is done from within, and employee satisfaction and retention is stellar. How did they get there? By committing to a gradual and transparent process that led to cross-functional growth, with top management driving the effort.

The 90 percent internal mobility rate of yore might be only a fond memory for this generation, but 50 percent is still batting .500—and that'll keep you in the game.

---

26 Business Insider, 2018.

THE BEST CANDIDATE SHOULD ALWAYS WIN

In the end, the best candidate—internal or external—wins. This said, I would argue in favor of treating your internal and external talent pools exactly the same, marketing to both groups frequently and strategically.

It's also important to set clear expectations around every job offering. SmartRecruiters always seeks to promote from within, but we'll never compromise on quality of hire. This may sound harsh, but setting and sticking to high expectations is key. The last thing you want to do is set your valued employees up for failure in roles for which they are not suited. Policies that give internal employees the right to view and apply for available jobs weeks *before* the external market do not facilitate a level playing field. It's better to prioritize fluidity and transparency to maximize opportunities.

KEY TAKEAWAYS

- Internal hiring brings many advantages, including lower risk and costs, better communication across company divisions, and reduced turnover.

- To maximize internal hiring volumes, make all job opportunities available to all employees, and remove any friction from the process.

- If you're not sure whether to market jobs to your own team, just remember that your competitors are marketing to them at this very moment.

CHAPTER 11

WHAT A GREAT
EXPERIENCE

When Graeme Johnson, the former head of resourcing at Virgin Media, set out to understand where his company stood on candidate experience (CandX), he was in for a surprise. As it turned out, a large portion of rejected candidates were highly dissatisfied with their application experience. To make matters worse, 18 percent of the unhappy former candidates were also Virgin Media customers—and 6 percent of them had since canceled their $60 monthly subscriptions. The result was devastating: a $5.4 million loss in revenue. Still, there was a bright side: Johnson got the green light to revamp the candidate experience at Virgin. Hundreds of employees were trained to provide a better candidate experience, the online application process was streamlined, and candidate satisfaction was monitored every step of the way. The result was a newly discovered $7 million revenue stream.[27]

The impact of candidate experience on your company's brand can't be overstated. Over 40 percent of people who experience poor treatment when applying for jobs report that they would decrease or fully sever relationships with that business. And who can blame them? Why would you buy from a company that treats you poorly?

Think about how many candidates your company processes every year, and who those people are—customers, partners, friends, referrals, suppliers. They are the people in your community whose opinions matter and whose business you absolutely want to retain. If you care about your bottom line and your company brand, it will serve you well to treat every one of those candidates like the customers they are.

THE BASICS OF GOOD CANDX

It's certainly important that your careers page should showcase the company culture, perks, diversity and inclusion information, and any other programs you offer. This will add heart and personality to your job ads, giving candidates a deeper

---

27 Inc., 2016.

sense of connection with your brand. Just remember that all the perks in the world won't sell a job that candidates can't find on your site.

LIST YOUR JOB

It's critical that all open jobs should be available in a single location on your careers page. Don't make candidates click around to different locations, subsidiaries, or even countries if you're a global company. Make jobs easy to search. The reason candidates visit your careers page is to find a job, so make finding a job easy.

MAKE IT EASY TO APPLY

Applying for a job online should be as seamless a process as completing a purchase on a retailer's website. At the very least, it requires clear, robust, and targeted information. Candidates should be able to apply from their desktop or phone, through your site or LinkedIn (both should be options), in a maximum of five minutes. To enable this, the application should allow for quick resume uploading, and avoid asking the candidate to type in copious amounts of information. If you can rent an apartment in Moscow for the weekend in two clicks, why can't you apply for a job in Moscow with two clicks?

ALWAYS RSVP

Are you interested in me or not? That's what candidates want to know after applying for a role. If a candidate manages to successfully apply, they should always receive a response from your company in the form of a confirmation email, at minimum.

Unfortunately, nearly 80 percent of applicants never hear anything after applying for a job. And when they do, it's usually via a heartless letter sent out by an outdated applicant tracking system. The traditional "We received your resume and will be in touch if your skills match our needs" afterthought can be forever banished from recruiting lexicon.

RESPECT EVERY CANDIDATE'S TIME

Your recruiting organization and the hiring manager or interview team never want to appear to take a candidate's time or goodwill for granted. For this reason alone it's important to avoid constant rescheduling, missed meetings, and late starts. Further, you'll want to make sure that your prescreeners are qualified to evaluate potential candidates, and your interviewers are well-prepared.

PROVIDE POSTINTERVIEW FEEDBACK

If you were to audit your company's interview protocol right now, I'd be willing to bet what you'd find: your organization does not consistently provide feedback after an interview. We've all been candidates at some point, which is why the "do unto others as you would have them do unto you" approach will always steer you correctly. In recruiting, this means transparency in the application process. Small things like notifications when a resume has been reviewed or another relevant position has opened up make a big difference.

The good news is, creating a positive candidate experience is straightforward. Make it easy to apply, respond to the applicant after they apply, communicate throughout the process, and provide postinterview feedback. A good talent acquisition suite can assist you with all of these steps—building courteous behavior into technological automation.

Now, if you're thinking: *There must be a shortcut to make my company look like a great employer. Can't I just fake it?* I'm afraid the answer is no. Your employer brand and candidate experience are being reviewed on a virtual worldwide stage. At this very moment, on platforms like Glassdoor, Google, and Yelp, your candidates and employees are being asked: "Were you treated properly? Was the interview difficult? Did they respond to you in time? What's it like to work at that company? How much do they pay?" More than 70 percent of job seekers read these online reviews prior to accepting or even applying for a role, which weighs heavily on your end results.

THE BENEFITS OF AN IMPECCABLE EXPERIENCE

A smooth candidate experience will enhance your business in ways that are too good to ignore. Here are the three main areas of impact:

IMPROVED SOURCING

Companies that provide an efficient and satisfying candidate experience attract more candidates, drive more referrals, receive 50 percent more qualified inbound applications, and see a higher response rate from direct sourcing. In fact, candidates are twice as likely to respond to a company email if they are already engaged with your brand, saving you 50 percent of your sourcing budget. That's one big incentive to step up your candidate game.

LOWER WITHDRAWAL RATES

Imagine you have three solid candidates for a plum role at your company, and one of them gets frustrated with your process and bails out. More often than not, that was the best person for the job—the candidate with the highest expectations and most options. Now, your silver medalist gets the nod, which means you're hiring the second best of the bunch. Although the fallout from losing a star performer can be difficult to measure, it carries significant impact. A seamless candidate experience means you're giving all you've got for the gold-medal candidate, every time.

SALARY SAVINGS

Avoid this vicious cycle: a bad candidate experience leads to a bad company brand, which leads to the company overpaying to attract new hires—by as much as 10 percent, according to a *Harvard Business Review* study. If you can save 10 percent of every new hire salary, that's probably more than your entire recruiting budget. And then there's the fact that a large majority of men and women won't join a company with a bad reputation in the first place.28 But the good news: it works the other way, too. A good candidate experience leads to a good company brand, which leads to more growth, profit, and promise for your company.

CRAFTING A GREAT CANDIDATE JOURNEY

Once you've cleaned up your systems and processes, it's time to take things up a notch, to *impress*. There are lots of great ways to offer an exceptional candidate experience, and they all revolve around making a candidate feel comfortable, special, and valued.

---

28 Corporate Responsibility Magazine, 2015.

Take Sycomore AM, a Paris-based asset management company rooted in sustainable investing. Interested candidates start the application process with a meeting, which includes a thorough introduction to the company and an opportunity to ask questions. This is not part of the evaluation process, so it helps candidates feel comfortable, perform better in their interview, and make an informed decision. Even if they don't accept or are not offered a position, the process leaves a positive lasting impression. It's essentially building an informational interview into the process for prospective talent, without putting the burden on them to initiate.

Buddy systems can also be very effective. At one large financial services company, each senior-level candidate is assigned a buddy who ensures they have a great interview experience. Candidates are welcomed at reception and escorted to a comfortable area to learn more about the interview process and meet the interviewers. The buddy checks in regularly throughout the day and touches base after the interview to answer any outstanding questions.

It's a simple and highly effective process that leaves candidates feeling special. Some companies even take it a step further. Accenture introduces their buddy system early in the process through the referral system. Candidates are encouraged to find someone they know already on the Accenture team and leverage this connection for a referral. If a candidate accepts a role, they have a known insider to help them navigate new waters.

When it comes to candidate perks, LinkedIn leads the pack. Candidates receive interview preparation material before their day on site. Upon arrival, they are gifted a "WelcomeIN" package filled with goodies to keep them fueled and alert throughout the day, and an iPad containing a welcome letter, the day's agenda, interviewers' LinkedIn profiles, and access to company blogs and videos on topics like "Bring Your Kids to Work" and "Team Outings." And it doesn't end there. Also included is a "Candidate Map" of the campus and a badge that distinguishes them from other visitors. Settling in to the process, they are taken on a food tour, since LinkedIn is known for offering the best office meals in Silicon Valley. After the eventful day, the interview panel is required to provide specific and constructive feedback within forty-eight hours. Ultimately, everything is done with a purpose: to show respect for the candidate.

BUILDING EMPLOYER BRAND

Beyond the transactional components of candidate experience is a much bigger animal: employer brand. Employer brand has a long reach, affecting talent attraction, engagement, and retention. The process of building your brand includes measuring and aiming to improve sixteen different company attributes, including benefits and perks, career advancement, change and stability, company reputation, corporate social responsibility, culture and values, diversity and inclusion, environment, workplace innovation, and technology.[29]

Your employer brand, of course, is deeply intertwined with your customer brand and your shareholder brand. As Connecticut-based Frontier Communications has found, it can sometimes be difficult to determine which is impacting which. As of 2019, Frontier has a Glassdoor employee satisfaction score of 2.5 out of 5—one of the lowest of any major American company. Just 24 percent of reviewers recommend working for the company and only 16 percent approve of the CEO. Coincidentally or not, the company's revenue and share price have spiraled downhill in recent years, falling from over $50 a share to less than $1.

Now let's look at how recruiting can be leveraged to *positively* impact your employer, customer, and shareholder brands.

A great example of this is the Heineken Group's 2019 GO Places campaign, featuring an interactive website that allowed applicants to seamlessly learn about the company culture. Among the site's features was a gamified personality quiz that

---

29 The Employer Brand Index.

revealed if an applicant was a pioneer, investigator, mediator, or initiator. The message: "At Heineken, you can design your own career." The campaign was wildly successful, resulting in a *300 percent* increase in applicants.

To boot, GO Places also directly communicated with employees, customers, and investors through tailored messaging. Heineken told current employees: "You work at one of the world's most creative companies." The customer message was: "We're the world's best brewery, with more than 250 beers in over 70 countries." Investors got the message: "We're going places."

Every facet of your brand benefits when you develop an exceptional, holistic recruiting campaign. Amplify impact by having your marketing and recruiting teams joined at the hip and working in sync. This builds a cohesive brand and drives results that go far beyond simple candidate attraction.

CREATING A KILLER CAREER SITE

The partnership between recruiting and marketing teams can really shine on your company's site. Of all the tools that candidates use to research new opportunities and inform their decision making, the corporate career site is the runaway winner, according to 65 percent of job seekers. By comparison, only 30 percent of candidates turned to LinkedIn pages and newsletters to learn about prospective employers.[30]

If the eyes are the windows to the soul, the careers page is the open door to a company's culture. Your careers page is where you confidently convey your company mission, purpose, values, and principles. This is the place to shout out your brand from the virtual rooftops. *Here's how some of the world's largest companies are expressing their personalities in this space:*

- **Spotify:** "Join the band." Succinct, inclusive, and exactly what you'd expect from them.

- **Airbnb:** "Create a world that inspires human connections." Perfectly suited to their brand and what they do.

- **Facebook:** "Do the most meaningful work of your career." Bold and full of promise.

- **Twitter:** "#love where you work." It lacks some purpose but promises happiness and ties directly to their signature, the hashtag.

- **Walmart:** "Don't just work harder, career better." An attempt at clever, but somewhat confusing.

---

30 The Talent Board, 2018.

- **Amazon:** "Come build Earth's most customer-centric company with us." Straightforward, clear, and inspiring.

An inspiring tagline is a huge win, but don't stop there. Your careers web page needs accessible and practical information about the company and its people, available career paths, and skills and development options. One word of caution: making a good first impression is important, but rein the impulse to use flowery marketing language. Be transparent, clear, and genuine. Candidates want real information, not a rant from your ad people.

Considering that 60 percent of traffic to your website gets there via mobile devices, it makes sense to keep your message short and sweet. Candidates visit your careers page because they are interested in a job; extraneous features may distract and contribute to visitors leaving the site without taking action.

A broken job-search experience is a losing scenario, plain and simple. It's not efficient for conversions, and it's like waving a flag to candidates announcing you're not quite all together. Job searches also must be fast, practical, and easy to do. Perhaps experiment with allowing candidates to drag and drop their resumes and receive suggestions on which jobs might best suit them. Make the search experience fulfilling and, most of all, productive.

And before candidates sign off, offer them a simple get-in-touch prompt: "Interested in exploring more opportunities with us? Sign up here and we'll be in touch." It only takes a few clicks for the candidate and is particularly effective for pipeline recruiting on your end.

MEASURING CANDIDATE EXPERIENCE AND EMPLOYER BRAND

We've discussed how important it is to dial in a rewarding candidate experience and build your employer brand. To help make that a success, here are some helpful metrics to track along the way.

TRACKING WEBSITE HIRES

Tracking the percentage of hires originating organically from your website is a solid indicator of your company's reputation and appeal, although it can be further influenced by specific advertising strategies.

MONITORING WITHDRAWAL RATE

What percentage of candidates making it through a phone screen interview actually end up withdrawing their application? That number is directly linked to the experience you provide, the speed of the process, and follow-up communication. Withdrawal rate should always remain well below 10 percent.

HOMING IN ON OFFER ACCEPTANCE

What percentage of extended offers is accepted? This ties directly back to candidate experience, interview quality, company reputation, and of course the attractiveness of the job package. Remember that if you are losing candidates through the process, you're likely losing the best ones. Extended offers should see an acceptance rate of more than 80 percent.

LISTENING TO CANDIDATE EXPERIENCE

Ask your candidates how they feel about the process. Even a simple survey after rejection or withdrawal says a lot. As Virgin Media learned to the tune of $5.4 million in recovered revenue, it *always pays to listen to your customers.*

KEY TAKEAWAYS

- Your employer, shareholder, and customer brands are joined at the hip. Consider how they can leverage one another.

- You can't fake a good candidate experience, but it's not difficult to do it right with an easy apply process, timely feedback, and just plain respect.

- An exceptional candidate experience is critical to your ability to convince the best talent to accept your offer.

- Build an engaging career website and keep it updated. The majority of your site traffic goes straight to the career page, so make it memorable for them.

PART THREE

THE ART (AND SCIENCE) OF SELECTION

CHAPTER 12

WAIT...WHAT ARE WE LOOKING FOR?

n chapter 2, I told you about a SmartRecruiters client, a large tech company that had made mistakes or mismatches on over half their hires. Bad hires, statistically, either leave in the first year, or worse, stick around in a state of mediocre productivity that demoralizes their coworkers. As we dug deeper to determine root cause, results showed that the majority of managers said they were disappointed with their low-rated employee's attitude, motivation, personality, or work ethic. On the candidate side, many said they didn't like their supervisor, or the culture was not what they had expected.

How could such an established company be so far off the mark with hiring? Did they have a sourcing problem? Not really;

this was a strong brand with a very healthy inflow of candidates, so the problem originated in the selection process. Could the problem be that they actually didn't know what they were looking for? Close, but not exactly. As it turned out, the heart of the tech company's recruiting conundrum was that they were hiring for aptitude—and ignoring attitude.

IF YOU HIRE FOR APTITUDE, YOU'LL FIRE FOR ATTITUDE

Roughly 90 percent of bad hires at U.S. companies can be traced back to bad employee attitude—lack of motivation, low emotional intelligence, unsuitable temperament, and other culture-fit issues.

That in turn raises a question: if we fire for attitude, should we not be screening for this rather than just for aptitude? In other words, is personality a better predictor of future performance than skills, education, experience, and past experience?

In early 1992, I was in the early stages of my career as a headhunter in Prague. The Soviet regime had recently crumbled, and the national economy was transitioning from a planned communist system to a liberal capitalist model. At the time, no one had any experience or education in business-relevant fields. This made recruiting challenging, to say the least. One of my clients was the global cosmetics giant, L'Oréal. To this day, I remember a telling conversation with the company's general manager:

"I need a marketing manager with a master's in marketing and five to ten years' experience in consumer goods or beauty," the manager told me.

"Sorry," I replied. "No one in this country has five years' experience in marketing."

"Okay, then just a marketing graduate with a good degree."

"No one here has a marketing degree from a university."

"Fine," the manager sighed. "Just find me someone who speaks English and can do the job."

As reductive as it sounds, the manager ended up giving me a great directive: to find him someone who'd get the job done. We needed to look beyond must-haves to the whole person behind the candidate.

MUST-HAVES VERSUS MUST-ACHIEVES

In traditional hiring models, we take a job description that lists all the tasks and responsibilities of a position and turn it into an "ideal candidate" profile. We then evaluate candidates against that ideal profile. What many employers end up with is a description of what I call a "purple squirrel," a rare-to-nonexistent dream candidate in possession of a long list of specific skills, achievements, and experiences. That model is completely flawed. Instead of must-haves, let's think about must-achieves. What type of personality and character is best-suited to carry out the tasks at hand? An effective way for companies to judge this is to examine their top staffers' character traits, then search for candidates who share those characteristics.

THE PERFORMANCE-BASED SCORECARD

At SmartRecruiters, we use a performance-based evaluation scorecard to ensure that we're evaluating candidates for attitude and desired performance rather than a laundry list of skillsets. One way we assess attitude is to ask whether a candidate "will demonstrate our values consistently" based upon situational case questions and prodding for examples as validation. And when it comes to desired performance, we care more about the applicant's *suitability* for fulfilling specific goals than how many of those milestones they've reached in the past. In other words, our internal-facing scorecard defines the work that needs to be done, not the history of the person doing it. It's an incredibly useful predictor of future performance. With the right scorecard, the right interview team, and accurate assessment, you minimize hiring mistakes.

Developing an efficient job scorecard isn't easy, however. The key to success is to make the task a collaborative effort between your recruiting/HR teams and the hiring manager. All involved parties should start by answering the question: "Do we really need this person, and what do we really need this person to achieve?"

This step is so important that, at SmartRecruiters, I set a rule that recruiting does not start until the scorecard is written. I personally validate each candidate scorecard and occasionally challenge my team when expectations for the role seem misaligned. Given that the scorecard is filled in by busy interview teams, I keep it relatively concise, with a range of six to ten criteria.

I recently went to market to hire a chief technology officer (CTO) for SmartRecruiters. That's a senior executive role reporting to me and overseeing the entire products and engineering team—about half the company. Here's what that interview scorecard looked like:

	Rating | 1=Strong No, 3=Maybe, 5=Strong Yes				
CTO Scorecard Criteria	1	2	3	4	5
Smartian Fit Will demonstrate our values consistently. (This is our standard culture fit. Exists in every scorecard.)					
Exceptional Team Builder, Mentor and Coach Will hire, develop and retain amazing talent and foster a culture of innovation.					
Exceptional Engineering Org & Process Will build a highly effective product and engineering organization with state of the art processes, clear ownership to achieve max velocity.					
Exceptional Product & UX Instincts Will synthesize complex problems into simple solutions resulting in elegant product requirements and consumer class usability.					
Visionary Architect and Tech Leader Will design clean architecture with the right logical granularity and make sustainable technology choices to ensure long-term maintainability and velocity.					
Deep Expertise in Enterprise Cloud Will manage the product life cycle in an enterprise Cloud business including roadmap management, hosting, SLA, security, communications, etc.					
Solid AI & Machine Learning Expertise Will leverage the power of AI and Machine Learning and build a data culture to accelerate our matching and conversational abilities.					

Note that the scorecard does not say, "We want an MIT or Stanford graduate with fifteen years' experience with a major SaaS company, at least five years' experience in a management role, and deep connections with industry leaders." That is not a candidate profile. A good profile outlines what the candidate must achieve and challenges your interview team to determine: is this *the* person for the job?

KEY TAKEAWAYS

- To ensure success, build a clear, job-specific scorecard to evaluate candidates against. Do not start hiring without it.

- Forget the must-haves. A performance-based scorecard focuses on the must-achieves, which is a much better lens through which to evaluate candidates.

- Balance skills and behaviors. Hiring based solely on aptitude almost always leads to firing for attitude.

CHAPTER 13

TELL ME ABOUT YOURSELF

B ack in 2009, two tech-savvy engineers, Brian Acton and Jan Koum, applied to work at Facebook but were turned down. Nonplussed, they redirected their efforts and started WhatsApp. Five years later, Facebook acquired WhatsApp for $19 billion—quite possibly the most expensive recruiting mistake ever made.

What happened? The recruiter didn't see potential? Were Acton and Koum not great fits at the time? Perhaps they didn't present their best selves during the interview? From the outside, it's hard to tell. What's clear, though, is how hard (some say broken) interviewing really is.

WHY UNSTRUCTURED INTERVIEWS DON'T WORK

A few years ago, the University of Texas Medical School at Houston was mandated to quickly fill fifty more seats than they'd planned for. With no time to spare and without further evaluation, the department admitted a round of candidates they'd previously rejected after the first round of interviews. A key point in this story is that the first and only interview round—which had resulted in the hiring of certain candidates and the rejection of others—had consisted of *unstructured* interviews. As opposed to a structured interview, in which questions are predetermined and asked in a standardized order, an unstructured interview is more like an informal conversation.

Fast-forward a few years, and the school saw no meaningful differences between the first-choice and second-choice students in terms of attrition, academic performance, clinical performance, or honors earned.

Time and again, in the realms of both academic admissions and job hiring, unstructured interviews have proven to produce unreliable outcomes. Why? Instead of fostering objective evaluation, they invite bias. What typically happens is a recruiter, HR staffer, or department manager has a chat with a candidate and exits the interview feeling they've met someone they like. Instead of evaluating whether the candidate will make a good accountant or project manager, interviewers unconsciously (or consciously in many instances) ask themselves if they like the person. They're confident in their judgment, though they may not have obtained any reliable evidence or indicator of future performance.

THE BIAS PROBLEM

We all have bias; it's inherent to human connection. We tend to connect better if we have something in common—we grew up in the same city, read the same books, play the same sport, believe in the same God, speak the same language, have a similar dress code, and so on. That's great when getting to know people as friends; but in interview situations, it's often unproductive and can lead to a variety of serious issues, from poor job performance to lost revenue.

We'll dig deeper into the problem of bias and how to overcome it in chapter 20. Here, we'll tackle the issue at the interview stage, where we can obtain relevant data to make an accurate and reliable screening decision.

MAKE THE MOST OF STRUCTURED INTERVIEWS

The best way to make sure you end an interview with precise and relevant information is to be prepared with precise and relevant questions. It sounds simple, but few interviewers actually do it.

For example, let's say I'm hiring for a sales rep. I approach the interview with a set of questions and a clear plan. Some of the questions are job-specific: "How would you go about building a territory plan to ensure you consistently hit quota?" Some questions are about skills and self-awareness: "What are your superpowers?" Or, for managers: "What does your latest 360 Assessment say, and what have you done about it?" To get a feel for whether the candidate has bothered to do their homework on the role and the company as a whole, I always ask, "What questions do you have for me?"

Each position commands a different set of questions, but the rule of thumb is: walk in with ten that you know you are going to ask, then let the rest of the interview unfold naturally so it doesn't feel like an interrogation. It helps to choose questions based on a scorecard like the one from the previous chapter, ensuring of course that it's tailored to the specific position.

HOW TO LEVERAGE THE WISDOM OF THE TEAM

While structured interview questions may help gather relevant information and limit bias, the best way to achieve accurate interview outcomes is to rely on multiple perspectives. To me, the best interview teams include at least three people: the hiring manager, a peer to the candidate, and someone from an adjacent department or role. The team needs to be diverse to ensure diversity of opinions. It can but does not absolutely need to include a representative from HR or recruiting.

I find peer interviews to be particularly illuminating. Peers make great interviewers because they know exactly what it takes to do the job. For example, a hiring manager interviewing for a retail position might ask typical mundane questions about a candidate's achievements or skills. A peer, on the other hand, will get right into it, asking, "Are you okay standing on your feet for eight hours a day?" This approach provides "real life" information for the candidate *and the interviewer.*

CLARIFY THAT INTERVIEWING IS A PRIVILEGE

How do you decide who will be part of the interview team? I believe anyone can be an interviewer as long as they recognize that interviewing is a privilege and should be seen as such. Convey to your interviewers that you are entrusting them with a highly significant undertaking. Let them know that their opinion matters. To that end, interviewers must have a clear understanding of what is involved. In exchange for the privilege of helping to choose their future colleagues, interview team members are expected to commit to two things: First, to be prepared, having thoroughly read the candidate's resume and written down their ten must-know questions. Second, to provide detailed and timely feedback. If an interviewer fails on either of these fronts, maybe they shouldn't interview for the company again.

REQUIRE TIMELY, STRUCTURED FEEDBACK

Along with structured questions, structured feedback is critical. In fact, tight collaboration between recruiters and hiring managers is the number-one indicator of high-performance hiring organizations.[31] While recruiters may gripe about low response rate and slow response times from hiring managers, the use of a scorecard system combined with technology that intuitively guides this process virtually eliminates such headaches. When an interview is complete, the interviewer is immediately reminded to fill in the scorecard with a rating of each of the core competencies defined for that role, as well as an overall review—exactly what you're looking for.

You can easily use the scorecard to compare and contrast candidates. And when two interviewers have different perspectives on a candidate, you can discern the exact points on which they differ, leading to healthy debate and further clarifications.

---

31 Bersin Academy, 2019.

AVOID GROUP-THINK

The question becomes: how do you avoid bias? Your interview team will, by nature, be made up of employees of varying levels. If a manager on the team likes a candidate, it's essential that this manager's subordinate feels empowered to disagree. To avoid unwanted influence, I recommend implementing a cards-down approach in which interviewers do not see one another's feedback until they have submitted their own. With unbiased feedback from all interviewers, you can reach a better decision.

YOU *CAN* FORCE OPINIONS

Understandably, some interviewers may be reluctant to share their opinions at all. It's easier to say, "I'm not sure," than to deliver what may be a risky or unpopular vote. But it's the interviewer's responsibility to show their cards, so to speak, and there's nothing wrong with forcing their hand if necessary. To that end, Google famously uses a four-star rating system, where four stars means "I will resign if we *don't* hire this person," and one star means "I will resign if we *do* hire this person."

RAISE THE BAR: A MAYBE IS A NO

A common question I hear is, "How do I know my managers are making good hiring decisions if I'm not interviewing every candidate myself?" It's a valid question, especially considering that 95 percent of managers surveyed admit they've hired candidates in spite of misgivings.[32] In hindsight, these managers sensed something was not quite right, but ignored their gut and moved forward anyway—to unhappy results.

And that leads us to a basic rule of thumb in recruiting: a maybe is a no. When analyzing scorecard feedback from different team members, any "maybe" is a clear signal to dig deeper. And often, the hiring team will start raising the bar for themselves.

Undoubtedly, interviewing works best as a collaborative effort. Teams working with structured scorecards and sticking to a disciplined process will produce much better hiring outcomes for your company.

We'll leave the last word on the importance of sky-high standards to Jeff Bezos, who said, "Setting the bar high in our approach to hiring has been and will continue to be the single most important element of Amazon's success." To achieve that, he challenges his interview teams to answer three questions about each new hire: Will this person raise the average level of effectiveness of the group they're entering? Will you admire this person? Along what dimensions will this person be a superstar?

---

32 Brandon Hall Group & Glassdoor, 2015.

The next Jeff Bezos might be interviewing with your team right now. Will they hire this person?

KEY TAKEAWAYS

- Unstructured interviews have no place in your hiring process. Be prepared with structured questions and an interview scorecard.

- The best way to achieve accurate interview outcomes is to rely on multiple perspectives from interview teams of at least three people.

- Interviewing is a privilege and should be seen as such. Select interviewers strategically. Peer interviews are particularly useful.

- Don't settle for maybes when evaluating a candidate. In recruiting, a maybe is a no.

CHAPTER 14

CANDIDATE TESTING

S ince the dawn of the labor market, employers have leveraged testing in the candidate selection process. In China's Tang Dynasty in 206 BC, aspiring bureaucrats were required to undergo a series of tests known as the Chinese imperial examinations. Exams were based on knowledge of the classics, which reflected the candidates' educational background and social class more than their suitability for the job. Without wealth and privilege, after all, one was more likely to have grown up laboring than reading great works of literature. And thus, the imperial hierarchy was reinforced and perpetuated.

PERSONALITY ASSESSMENT

Historically, candidate testing was focused on knowledge. But today, the more egalitarian practice of personality assessment is more common. Many employers have shifted from testing concrete attributes like English-speaking competency to testing less tangible traits like patience and empathy. Behavioral science allows us to accurately evaluate which prospects are the best psychological fits for our companies, to help people determine their best career paths, to quickly refine a candidate pool, and even to predict how long a candidate is likely to stay in a role based on emotional stability. I recently met with a company that sought to lower their employee turnover rate across two thousand stores by improving new hire suitability. They used a personality assessment tool during the interview process to compare candidate results against top-performing employee behavioral traits and to identify top matches. After eighteen months and over ten thousand hires, the company found that this testing process effectively boosted new employee retention by 19 percent, saving them millions of dollars.

One of the most widely used models for testing personality is the Myers–Briggs Type Indicator (MBTI), developed in the early twentieth century by Katharine Cook Briggs and her daughter Isabel Briggs Myers. The MBTI is based on a conceptual theory of psychological types proposed by the renowned psychiatrist Carl Jung. The system defines a person's personality through four opposing functions: extraversion versus introversion, sensing versus intuition, thinking versus feeling, and judging versus perception. Once you've decided which style you identify with on each of the four functions, you create a four-letter code, which sums up your type. For example, an ESTJ would be someone with a preference for extraversion, sensing, thinking, and judging.

A side note: Katharine Cook Briggs began her personality trait research upon meeting her future son-in-law. She had observed marked differences between his personality and that of other family members, sparking a drive to find out if he would be a good match for her daughter. Little did she know that her research would evolve from evaluating love to predicting job performance.

An assessment's ability to predict future job performance is called a validity coefficient. In general, validity coefficients range from 0 to .50, where 0 is poor validity and .50 is moderate validity. Most modern personality assessments fall within this range, meaning they are moderate indicators of candidate suitability at best. The takeaway: in job matching, as in dating, there's no such thing as a sure thing. So, test in conjunction with interviewing, not in place of it.

BENCHMARKING TOP PERFORMERS

In high-volume hiring settings such as sales call centers, personality assessment can be useful for evaluating candidates against star performers. What do the top 10 to 20 percent of agents have in common that we are looking for? Which qualities are essential for top performers in our specific organization? It's almost like cloning your best talents. Using this assessment approach, one telecom company increased their revenue per call by 74 percent, a huge net gain.[33]

TESTING HELPS DIVERSITY

Whether you're evaluating your candidates for attitude or asking them to complete good old-fashioned programming tests, the results can lead to rewarding gains in diversity for your team. As I mentioned earlier in the book, recruiters and interviewers have a natural tendency to replicate, meaning to look for candidates with similar characteristics, interests, and experiences as their own. In doing so, they narrow the talent pool and may exclude high-quality candidates who may not fit "the norm." Assessments, on the other hand, evaluate people's attributes, behavior, and skills—helping to deemphasize the importance of titles and credentials. Generally speaking, in the world of recruiting, assessments help even the playing field.

---

33 SMG Academy, 2017.

VALUING YOUR CANDIDATE'S TIME

Testing is so easy and automated these days that many organizations have a tendency to over-test. This puts an unfair and unnecessary burden on candidates. Imagine applying to twenty companies and being asked to do an hour of testing for each. Don't test just for the sake of testing, and beware of irrelevant testing.

I recently encountered a company that was using a numerical reasoning test to evaluate graphic designers. The test had no relevance to the position and was just there as a habitual part of the process. Only when a top designer candidate refused to take the test did the company finally question its process. It's always a good time to reevaluate *your* process and ask: "Are we doing the right tests, for the right reasons? Is what we are asking reasonable?"

A good rule of thumb is to start small. Offer shorter, general tests early in the process, and move to longer, more involved tests for finalists. For example, you might ask a sales representative candidate to take a five-minute gamified personality assessment upon application. By the time they are in the final stages, they would have a half-day job simulation (a common hiring component in many of today's tech jobs) with role playing to evaluate their ability to build and deliver a structured sales pitch. Ultimately, this is all about the context and the importance of the role.

PRETESTING

In recent years, standardized testing platforms have started to appear, allowing candidates to validate their skills even before applying for the job. On open networks like Coding Games and Hacker Rank, candidates can build a profile with validated skills that companies trust, thus saving them the time of taking a different test for every employer. This is an efficient way to go, particularly with software developer roles.

I suspect that this trend will continue to develop, with the old resume ultimately being replaced by a blockchain-protected digital profile that includes pretested skills, personality type, background checks, and more. Without a doubt, the science of assessment will continue to evolve, becoming ever more essential to the candidate selection process.

KEY TAKEAWAYS

- Testing is a science that can deliver meaningful returns and make the variables of selection more constant.

- While testing is a powerful tool, it's not a silver bullet; it should only be used in conjunction with interviewing, not in place of it.

- By testing candidates' attributes, behavior, and skills and deemphasizing the importance of titles and credentials, bias is reduced and rewarding gains in diversity can be achieved.

CHAPTER 15

PLEASE ACCEPT
MY OFFER

n 1983, Steve Jobs was looking for a president for his company. After an extensive search, he and the Apple board decided to extend an offer to John Sculley, then-president at PepsiCo, a much bigger company than Apple at the time. Sculley initially declined the offer but Jobs didn't give up, pressing his dream candidate with the now famous line, "Do you want to sell sugar water for the rest of your life, or do you want to come with me and change the world?" Sculley accepted the offer.

OFFER MANAGEMENT

The Apple story reminds us that if recruiting is about marketing and selling, offer management is about closing. Let's say you've found the perfect candidate for your job and she is clearly the best fit; why take a chance on losing her? If you do, you'll be forced to hire the second-best candidate, or worse, to start over. Companies typically operate at an offer acceptance rate of about 70 percent in a competitive market and 80 to 85 percent in less competitive segments. Improving that ratio naturally will help you ensure that you're consistently hiring the best.

Securing the best hires involves timing. Take too long and your candidate could be gone. In fact, roughly 40 percent of candidates who refuse offers do so because another opportunity presented itself in the interim.

If your company struggles with extended hiring processes, it's an easy fix that starts with automating your offer management. A smart software will ensure that as soon as the decision to hire has been made, the process continues forward. Preparing, approving, and submitting an offer should never take more than a week, and ideally just one or two days in competitive markets.

MAKE IT MEMORABLE

Accepting a new job is a major decision for a candidate, as well as their family. Fear of the unknown is a powerful obstacle to acceptance, and to allay that fear, make that offer too memorable and too good to refuse.

One Spotify recruiter recently sent a candidate an offer letter in the form of a playlist titled "We Need You." Song titles on the list conveyed to the candidate that Spotify thought they were awesome and ardently wanted them to join the team. Simple, yet smart and quirky—and perfectly on-brand.

Another novel tactic in an increasingly digital world is to send a physical offer package to the candidate's home. The package can contain job documentation, informational material about the company, a handwritten note from the hiring manager, and even some goodies—anything that extends a warm welcome and fosters a sense of belonging.

At Atlassian, candidates receive a welcome package within forty-eight hours of receiving a verbal offer. The package includes an inspiring poem from the company's president, relating what it's like to be an Atlassian employee, as well as assorted incentives such as vacation trip vouchers. Recruiters also have the option to personalize packages for specific candidates. One candidate received two VIP concert tickets with her job offer because she had mentioned her husband was a huge fan of the band.

ALWAYS CALL

It should go without saying, but many managers don't bother to do this, so here goes: always follow up offers with a call to the candidate. Offer letters have their place, but they're formal documents and can be intimidating in tone and content. A verbal walkthrough, however, lends a personal touch that offers an opportunity to counter objections and steer the candidate toward the right decision.

Once your offer has been extended, it's time to close the deal.

EXPECT TO NEGOTIATE

In my early days as a headhunter, I once submitted an offer to a candidate for a senior sales position. The offer was solid, he accepted, and I excitedly called my client to share the good news. The client's first response was to ask if the candidate had negotiated the salary offer. I told the client that no, the candidate was pleased with the package and accepted off the bat. What happened next took me by surprise. "Well, if he doesn't negotiate his own salary," said my client, "how can I expect him to negotiate deals for us?" And then the client directed me to rescind the offer. In retrospect, I think he may have been right to do so. Great candidates typically have plenty of options and as a result will often negotiate any offer. If a candidate doesn't negotiate, what does that tell you? Either you've offered too much, or they have no alternative. Negotiation is a healthy part of the hiring process. Be prepared for it.

TRUST BUT VERIFY

Nobody wants to be lied to. Unfortunately, in recruiting it happens every day. According to HireRight, an employment screening company, 84 percent of candidates somewhat misrepresent or outright lie on their resume. This is a risk at every level. When the board of Yahoo appointed Scott Thompson as its CEO, they had no idea he had lied about obtaining a degree in computer science from Massachusetts Stonehill College. In a similar scandal, Kenneth Lonchar, then CEO of Veritas Software, lied about having an MBA from Stanford. Then there was Ramesh Tainwala, who was forced to quit as CEO of Samsonite after falsely claiming to have a doctorate in business administration. And in a particularly egregious case of resume-padding, RadioShack CEO David Edmondson was ousted for claiming not one but two impressive degrees when he had none.

These examples illustrate the importance of blending trust with verification. But how do you verify a candidate's information, short of hooking them up to a lie detector? Fortunately, polygraph testing is regulated to specific situations and recruiting is not one of them. There are, however, efficient methods available for conducting background checks. Most background screening services will confirm education and experience and check criminal records. With that step complete, you can move on to checking references.

THE REFERENCE CHECK

The best way to validate a candidate's performance record is to check references with previous employers. While this can be time consuming, I always conduct reference checks myself for staff reporting directly to me. I ask for three or four references who know the person well and spend fifteen minutes on the phone with each. People giving references typically want to be positive, so I usually have to dig a little to fully validate my evaluation and uncover pertinent information.

One question I like asking is, "On a scale of one to ten, where ten is perfect, where would you rate this person's performance?" If I get a seven or an eight response, it prompts the follow-up question of, "What would it take for the candidate to be a ten in your eyes?" The answer is always illuminating.

OFFER ACCEPTED!

The best candidates take convincing, but they're worth it. Sometimes the process makes the difference. Sometimes the offer package makes the difference. Sometimes, as with Steve Jobs' entreaty to John Sculley, you have to find what resonates. In any case, optimizing your offer process is an investment worth making. Now, go get them!

KEY TAKEAWAYS

- Time is of the essence. Try to submit offers in one or two days, and never more than a week, to ensure that a plum candidate doesn't accept an offer somewhere else.

- Make job offers memorable. Tailor them to the candidate when possible and include personalized touches to show the candidate you care.

- Always follow up with a call, and be prepared for the best candidates to negotiate.

- Trust your candidates to a point, but always verify. Conduct background checks and then follow up with reference checks.

CHAPTER 16

LET'S GET
STARTED

N o institution takes onboarding more seriously than the military, where new recruits are conditioned to forgo their individuality for the greater good of their units. I learned this as a young officer overseeing recruit training in the French paratroops. Every sixty days, a new batch of young civilian recruits would come under my charge, and it was my job to turn them into war-ready soldiers. The process started with giving the recruits standard uniforms, haircuts, and service numbers—making their appearance as uniform as possible. This was followed by intensive drills and imposed collective hardships that cemented the candidates' socialization into the military. It was fascinating to observe the young people under my charge morph into a cohesive unit, ready to obey orders and possibly sacrifice their lives.

I'm not suggesting hazing your new hires, but rather illustrating that onboarding can be a powerful tool. Facebook engineers, for instance, participate in a six-week boot camp that provides an intensive deep-dive into the company's culture, technology stack, and overall mission to "connect the world."

Each company will take a unique approach to onboarding, but some challenges are universal. Let's take a look at a few of them.

PREBOARDING: FROM YES TO DESK

There's a pervasive problem in hiring today: no-shows. Imagine you've undertaken the arduous recruiting process, painstakingly chosen the perfect candidate, and waited weeks to months for their start date. Then on their first day, they're a no-show. Over 25 percent of new hires back out of offers or just don't show up, according to a 2019 new employee study by the staffing firm Robert Half.

So how do you get from "yes" to desk? What does it take?

ANTICIPATE THE COUNTEROFFER

For starters, assume that your candidate's current employer will fight their resignation. Over 80 percent of high-potential candidates report receiving a counteroffer, and 15 percent of them accept.[34] Resigning is a difficult and emotionally charged step. Leaving one's familiar job and trusted colleagues to step into the unknown of a new role takes courage. In that moment of vulnerability, it's undeniably tempting for a candidate to retreat back to safety. This is why you must stay in touch with the candidate in the days after they've accepted your offer. A phone call is a must. Ask: "Did you resign already? How did it go? Did you talk to your family about making a switch? Are they supportive?" You get the idea.

AUTOMATE THE LOGISTICS

Let's say you safely survive the counteroffer. What's next? Get the paperwork and the logistics out of the way. The candidate will need to work with your team to tend to a slew of details before the first day—from finalizing a formal contract to setting up payroll preferences to procuring a company ID. To quickly move through these steps, it's worth investing in mobile-friendly platforms that automate them digitally. You want this to be an easy, seamless process for new hires, as well as an efficient use of your company resources.

---

34   Bramwith Consulting, 2018.

ACCELERATE LEARNING

The key here is continued engagement. So, once the logistics have been attended to, I recommend engaging new talent in a preboarding learning curriculum. What can the candidate read and watch to feel more connected to their new job? This might include presentations, event videos, blog posts, marketing materials, company overviews, and books about the industry. Not only will this accelerate their future contribution, but it will ensure continuous contact. And the results can be meaningful. One large, Indian insurance company found that introducing a sales preboarding program sped up induction time from seven to two days, accelerating lead generation by 35 percent.

JUMP-START TEAM CONNECTIONS

Lastly, it's critical to foster a sense of belonging in your new hire. Introducing them to the team early is great for morale and dramatically decreases the odds of a first-day no-show. When people resign, they leave behind friends and personal connections. The value of rebuilding these early cannot be overstated. At Twitter, for example, the team hosts a happy hour with senior leadership and a Friday afternoon projects presentation for new hires. At minimum, the hiring manager must invite the new hire out to coffee or lunch.

New hires greatly appreciate being included in planned team outings. Stay in touch. Make them feel welcome.

SHOULD YOU INVEST IN ONBOARDING AUTOMATION?

If you hire at least a hundred people a year, automating the process is strongly recommended. If you're a giant, hiring on a grand scale, automating can save you millions. General Electric, for instance, had their shared-services team deploy an automated solution to replace an outdated, homegrown, paper-based onboarding system. According to Nucleus Research, this saved them $3.7 million by simply reducing processing costs. Not accounted for were the massive savings that naturally came from an improved new hire experience—a significant reduction in no-shows and first-year turnover.

So, congratulations: your logistics are complete, and your new hire just walked through the door excited, engaged, and ready for real recruit training. Now, how do you make sure that your organization achieves *consistent* hiring success, at scale? In part 4, I'll tell you about how to assemble your dream hiring team, the secret to a seamless operating framework, a solid strategy for navigating compliance challenges, and much more.

KEY TAKEAWAYS

- Create a dynamic preboarding program to reduce the risk of no-shows.

- Stay in touch with the candidate in the days after they've accepted your offer. A phone call is a must. Anticipate the counteroffer.

- Invest in a mobile-friendly onboarding platform to automate new-hire paperwork and logistics.

- Foster a sense of belonging in your new hire by introducing them to your team *before* their first day on the job.

PART FOUR

HIRING SUCCESS AT SCALE

CHAPTER 17

THE TALENT ACQUISITION DREAM TEAM

We want the best of the best to come to Google, we
budget what it takes to find the best of the best.

—Todd Carlisle, Director of staffing, Google

When asked what a first-rate recruiting program looks like, people often point to Google, where you'll find about sixteen recruiters for every thousand employees. Most Fortune 500 companies employ just *two* recruiters per thousand employees. Why does Google invest eight times more heavily in their recruiting staff? They must receive thousands of unsolicited resumes every year, after all. The answer is actually simple: Google, like many high-performing businesses, recognizes that recruiting is a competitive function. Just as businesses invest in marketing in order to attract the best customers, they must invest in recruiting in order to attract the best talent.

If your competitors invest in recruiting, and you don't, they will continually out-hire you, and outpace you in the marketplace. It's not one individual hire, but the repeated, competitive out-hiring, over the long term, that separates companies. Look at Google versus Motorola, for instance. Google consistently out-hires Motorola. Guess who bought—then sold—whom in the end? Which do you want to be?

HOW TO ACHIEVE HIRING SUCCESS AT SCALE

We have learned how to attract great candidates, select the right ones, and hire them. But how do you achieve this at scale? Making a few good hires is easy; doing it consistently is considerably less so. The key: make the variables of recruiting constant by developing systems that provide a continual great pool of candidates, and a reproducible methodology for evaluating them. In other words, predictable success at scale will require a good mix of people, processes, and technology. First, let's talk about those people—specifically, your hiring managers.

MANAGERS (NOT RECRUITERS) OWN HIRING SUCCESS

It's time to banish the myth that recruiters own hiring success. Let's be clear: *managers* own hiring success. If the vice president of sales doesn't deliver their quota, they might try to blame marketing, but the truth is, you will hold them accountable. The same is true in hiring. If a vice president of sales can't hire great salespeople, don't let them blame recruiting. It's their job. They're accountable. This is actually one of their most important responsibilities, and it is what defines them as a leader.

All too often, though, managers relinquish the hiring responsibility to recruiters. They sit back, relax, and wait for that purple squirrel they requested—all the while getting more and more frustrated. However, when you think about it, recruiting is the only service that HR delivers to the managers. Everything else, managers usually deliver for HR. That means recruiting needs to be done right, because it is the brand of the chief human resources officer inside the organization. Otherwise, the human resources team wants to talk to the manager about strategic talent management and long-term workforce development, but this goes nowhere. Primarily because managers only want to discuss one thing: where are my candidates?

This is not right. The key to hiring success is to make your leadership own it. How do you achieve this? Measure the success of the executive team against key hiring metrics: net-hiring score and hiring velocity. Are we getting the people we need, and are they any good?

MANAGERS NEED RECRUITERS

While managers must own hiring in their departments, they cannot be successful at hiring alone. It's a team effort. Asking them to work in a vacuum would be akin to asking your sales team to succeed without any marketing support: they'd fail. Without recruiters on the team—the marketers in this scenario—the results would be dismal: low velocity (empty seats) and a low net-hiring score (mediocre hires), or both.

Unfortunately, this is how many organizations operate. Talent acquisition is treated as a cost center, with a perpetually tightening budget. You now have an underpaid, understaffed, and underappreciated talent acquisition team. As a result, these recruiting teams are pigeonholed to engage in reactive, tactical recruiting—the "post and pray" approach to hiring. There's no strategy, no defined process, and no consistent candidate experience.

The result of saving on recruiting is inevitably similar to the result of saving on marketing: small, short-term gains will be undercut by large, long-term losses. And even short-term gains are questionable, since, ironically, organizations that underfund their recruiting functions must then pay top dollar to outsource hiring to agencies.

Organizations with robust, mature talent acquisition teams, on the other hand, bring in 18 percent more revenue and 30 percent more profit than their low-maturity counterparts.[35] Undoubtedly, over the long term, hiring choices separate good companies from great ones.

So, let's look at what a mature talent acquisition function looks like.

TALENT ACQUISITION IS AN EVOLVING FUNCTION

Pat Gallagher, chairman, president, and CEO of the global insurance brokerage Gallagher, knew he needed the best of the best in insurance-sales talent for his company to thrive. But it's notoriously hard to hire great insurance agents and brokers at scale. Realizing that old-school recruiting wouldn't cut it, Gallagher shook things up, creating a different kind of talent acquisition team. He aligned with his chief human resources officer and vice president of talent acquisition to hire salespeople, rather than human resource experts, as

---

35   Bersin by Deloitte, 2018.

recruiters. Then, they backed this plan up with solid marketing and sourcing. Finally, Gallagher measured the success of his talent acquisition team not by the dusty old metrics of time-to-fill or cost-per-hire, but by the significant revenue generated by their new hires.

As Gallagher understood, a world-class talent acquisition department looks strikingly similar to a stellar sales and marketing department. It excels in the following three areas:

1. **Marketing:** A talent acquisition function must be excellent at attracting, engaging, nurturing, and converting a healthy pipeline of great candidates. The team will then offer candidates an amazing interview experience that elevates the company brand.

2. **Business alignment:** The talent acquisition team must partner closely with the hiring manager through a deep collaboration that drives the right hiring decisions. By demonstrating a thorough understanding of the talent market and the business challenges at hand, the talent acquisition team becomes a trusted advisor for the hiring manager—helping her express clear requirements, pick the right candidates, and close them.

3. **Operational excellence:** The recruiting function should be managed like a well-oiled machine, in control of all

processes, data, and projects, with proper forecasting, reliable delivery, and seamless compliance.

It may seem simple, but this is quite far from what traditional human resources and recruiting functions are used to. The main evolution here? The skillset.

THE MAIN ROLES IN MODERN RECRUITING

Over the last decade, the recruiting function has matured significantly. Historically, companies launched without dedicated recruiting. As a result, human resources generalists picked up the task of recruiting. Then, as companies expanded, the recruiting function developed to include proper, dedicated recruiters—usually from staffing agencies—with a focus on "placements," filling seats fast and cheap.

Several trends today are evolving talent acquisition functions toward more specialized, sophisticated roles. Recently, driven by LinkedIn, outbound sourcing appeared on the scene as the new gold standard in recruiting. As a result of LinkedIn's dominance in the hiring market, inbound recruiting—marketing your brand to attract candidates—has fallen out of favor. As discussed earlier, I believe that both have their merits. I also support the shift toward marketing being made by companies like Twitter, who are hiring "talent experience managers" to focus solely on optimizing the candidate experience.

Let's take a closer look at the main functions of a modern talent acquisition organization.

MARKETING

Marketers deliver prospects. They are in charge of all lead generation, your pipeline. Their job is to deliver a large pool of amazing, interested talent. They own all the programs and mass channels, like the company website, referrals, and advertising and marketing campaigns. They live and breathe your company brand. No recruiting skills are required of them, just straightforward digital marketing experience. You may want to hire this talent from your marketing department. The marketers on your recruiting team do not interact directly with candidates. This is a one-to-many model—one marketer generates and nurtures hundreds, even thousands, of prospective candidates.

SOURCING

Sourcers build shortlists of qualified, interested candidates. The junior people on the team qualify inbound applicants through prescreening. The senior sourcers handle more outbound research, meaning they make as many calls as it takes to find the best of the best. If the marketers do a good job, they are fishing in a barrel (a pool of warm prospects); if not, they are hunting in the open ocean (LinkedIn). Think of your sourcers as the equivalent of sales development representatives. They actually need limited recruiting or human resources knowledge. It's about resilience, and the ability to "smile when you dial." Sourcers prospect all day long, work one-on-one, and talk to candidates directly. This is a great breeding ground for future recruiters or salespeople in your organization.

COORDINATING

Coordinators support logistics. While many of the tasks they handle are gradually becoming automated, they are still key to centralizing your recruiting effort. Their tasks include interview scheduling, travel arrangements, onboarding, and coordination, to name a few. They will usually work out of a shared services center.

RECRUITING

Recruiters close deals. A far cry from the old-fashioned recruiter who was run ragged from wearing too many hats, the modern recruiter is a trusted talent advisor who understands the business's needs as well as the talent market as a whole. Recruiters are a bridge between the overall talent acquisition team and the hiring managers, with whom they work hand in hand to hire great talent on demand. They must be mentally aligned *and* physically close to the business. Otherwise, the partnership doesn't work.

Think of recruiters as your business partners. They understand the market. Their opinion matters. They help define what talent is needed and play a critical role, not only in selecting the right candidate, but in accompanying them all the way to the finish line. Additionally, they manage the sourcers, ensuring a fluid process and a healthy pipeline of candidates and coordinators.

Contrary to the current standard, I think recruiters need to be "bar raisers" and should not be incentivized to fill jobs quickly. If they can rely on sourcers to find candidates and on coordinators to support the process, then you will have a rich collaboration. On the other hand, if recruiters are expected to do *everything*—from being strategic partners to cold-calling candidates to scheduling interviews—the system will break down.

OPERATIONS

The recruiting operations team, sometimes called Rec Ops, is responsible for scaling your recruiting function. As talent acquisition becomes more sophisticated and digitized, it's important to have a proper Rec Ops team to handle systems, processes, insights, and enablement. Think of them as a modern Sales Ops team. In addition to owning the core system, the talent acquisition suite, they analyze data, prepare reports, offer insight, and otherwise enable your teams and managers to drive efficiency at scale. They also own privacy and compliance, which we'll cover in depth in chapter 19.

By now you should have a clear picture of what goes into assembling a dynamic and well-rounded talent acquisition team. In the next chapter, we'll further explore the relationship between the talent acquisition team and hiring managers, and how they can hold each other accountable.

KEY TAKEAWAYS

- Managers own hiring success and should be accountable for hiring velocity, while recruiters can own net hiring score.

- High-performing talent acquisition functions excel at candidate attraction, are deeply aligned with the business, and operate flawlessly.

- In the modern talent acquisition team, recruiters are trusted business partners supported by marketers, sourcers, and coordinators.

- The new Rec Ops function handles systems, processes, insights, and enablement to drive efficiencies and scalability.

CHAPTER 18

AN OPTIMAL RECRUITING MODEL

Eighty percent of CEOs put hiring top talent as their number-one priority.[36] The same is surely true for hiring managers. For them, the impact of poor hires and unfilled roles can be much more immediate. Like a short-staffed restaurant manager, the hiring manager often directly bears the brunt of job vacancies, taking on extra work and answering for mistakes or missed deadlines.

As a manager, your hires define you as a leader. Without the right team, managers may fail to deliver professionally and suffer personally—their work-life balance disrupted for months on end. Viewed through this lens, it's hardly surprising that

---

36 PwC CEO Survey, 2017.

many managers don't trust their recruiting partners. There's a real disconnect here: 80 percent of recruiters think they are staying on top of vacant roles, while 60 percent of managers believe their colleagues do *not* have a good grasp on their responsibilities.[37] It works both ways: while managers may believe recruiters are useless and out of touch, recruiters may view managers as lazy and unrealistic in their demands.

Undoubtedly, the hiring manager-recruiter relationship is somewhat broken, and hiring success cannot be achieved until it is fixed. The first step toward building a great relationship between managers and recruiters can be to ask: "What are managers best at, and where do they need recruiters' support? What can managers *realistically* expect from the talent acquisition function?" Let's take a look at how the relationship works at key steps in the recruiting process.

WHERE MANAGERS NEED HELP

INTAKE MEETING

At the start of the process is the intake meeting, wherein the hiring manager and recruiter sit down together to gather the requirements of the job, define a sourcing strategy, and build a job-specific scorecard. Managers can define requirements

---

37 Bersin by Deloitte, 2014.

alone, but they often lack the structure to do it well, which leads to floating requirements and an elongated process. Hence, this step needs to be standardized with templates and should ideally be supported by the talent acquisition team.

CANDIDATE ATTRACTION

This is where we are generating a healthy pipeline of interested candidates. To put it bluntly, managers themselves are bad at sourcing candidates. They simply don't have the time and expertise to attract and convert candidates. Lack of quality candidates in the pipeline means they may be inclined to hire the first acceptable choice, which of course leads to quality issues. This is why talent acquisition must own candidate attraction and deliver a long list of amazing candidates to choose from.

PRESCREENING

In this step, resumes are filtered and prescreening calls conducted to get to a shortlist of candidates ready for interviews. Managers can of course review resumes, pick the candidates they want to invite for interviews, and make screening calls— especially with assistance from modern AI tools. However, this remains a time-consuming process that can be greatly streamlined with support from the recruiter.

INTERVIEW SCHEDULING

At this point, schedules are coordinated and interviews are organized. The volume of interviews can be large, making this a time-consuming process. Nobody likes scheduling interviews, but the task has a critical impact on hiring velocity and candidate experience and should be closely attended to—just not by the manager. Coordinators on the talent acquisition team should take the reins here, with the assistance of good automation and centralization.

INTERVIEWING CANDIDATES

With the right selection process, scorecard, and assessments, managers and the hiring team can come to a high-quality selection without a recruiter. Contrary to common practices, this is a step where recruiter support is a "nice to have," but it's not critical, except in the case of high-impact roles.

CANDIDATE MANAGEMENT

Good candidate management is about hand-holding the process, following up with candidates, and driving the hiring team toward a decision. Managers generally do not excel at managing this process. And that's understandable: it's just not their job. So, they don't follow up, and they tend to leave candidates hanging. All too often in a competitive market, those candidates are lost to other jobs. For this reason, the recruiter should absolutely take the reins on candidate management.

OFFER MANAGEMENT

At this stage, the offer is made and negotiations begin. If offers are automated, the manager can trigger this step. But closing candidates is a core skill that many managers lack. They simply don't like to beg or negotiate. Thus, it's good to have a middleman. Introducing recruiters into this process adds tremendous value, especially for high-impact and/or high-scarcity roles.

PREBOARDING

Post-acceptance, it's time for preboarding. This process should be centralized and automated as much as possible to ensure efficiency and consistency. Managers play a role here, but the process is primarily driven by the talent acquisition team.

PRIORITIZING YOUR TALENT ACQUISITION RESOURCES

Now that we know what managers can expect from recruiters at every step of the hiring process, let's look at which hires require the biggest investment of your talent acquisition resources as a whole. Since not all jobs are created equal, it makes sense to devote more of your recruiting resources to talent that is scarce and/or high impact.

- **Core staff:** These candidates do not have specialized skills and are in large supply, so this is likely the lowest area of investment. The most important role for the talent acquisition team to play here is in candidate attraction, managing advertising budgets to ensure a solid stream of inbound applicants. It's nice if the talent acquisition team can prescreen candidates and schedule interviews, but managers can do this, too, especially nowadays with intelligent resume screening and self-scheduling. Further down in the process, recruiters should not be expected to participate in candidate interviews. Instead, they should focus on automating the offer-to-hire process so that everything runs smoothly once the hiring decision has been made.

- **Professionals:** These candidates are also easy to find but have a higher impact on the business, so it's nice for the recruiter to be present at the intake meeting for these roles. Candidate attraction is similarly important. But here, prescreening and interview scheduling become more important, because you want a better candidate experience. Interviewing candidates, however, remains optional, provided that a good scorecard has been built and the hiring team is set up for success. Finally, recruiters should play a central role in candidate management for professional roles.

- **Specialists:** This is a high-scarcity pool. As a result, candidate attraction is a must-have commitment for recruiters. Areas of importance include prescreening, interview scheduling, and interviewing candidates. Recruiters should also handle candidate management, from hand-holding to the offer to preboarding. If recruiters don't stay highly engaged with these rare candidates all the way to the finish line, managers might lose their first-choice hires.

- **Unicorns:** The high-impact, high-scarcity category is where the talent acquisition team really needs to be in the lead from start to finish. Recruiter support is a must-have at almost every step of the process, particularly during sourcing (which usually requires deep efforts); interviewing (partnering with the hiring team to help drive the right decision); candidate management (hand-holding each candidate with special care); and offer management (supporting the negotiation and closing the offer).

For further clarity, the recruiter's commitments to her manager are broken down in the following model:

RECRUITERS' COMMITMENTS TO HIRING MANAGERS

Service levels scale

Not needed	Nice to have
Important	MustHave

	Core	Professionals	Specialists	Unicorns
Intake meeting Gather requirements and build job specific scorecard.	Not needed	Nice to have	Important	MustHave
Candidate Attraction Generate a healthy pipe of interested candidates.	Important	Important	MustHave	MustHave
Prescreening Filter through resumes, conduct prescreening calls. Build Shortlist.	Nice to have	Important	Nice to have	MustHave
Interview Scheduling Coordinate schedules and organize interview.	Nice to have	Important	Important	Important
Interviewing Candidates Actual recruiter being part of the interview team.	Not needed	Important	Important	MustHave
Candidate Management Handholding the process, following up with candidates, driving towards a decision.	Nice to have	Important	MustHave	MustHave
Offer Management Issuing and negotiating the offer.	Nice to have	Important	MustHave	Important
Preboarding Following up post acceptance until Day 1.	Nice to have	Important	MustHave	Important

GOOD RECRUITING TAKES GOOD PLANNING

Once a hiring manager knows what to expect from her recruiters, her next question is often: how fast can I get my candidates?

The most efficient way to deliver those candidates is not by racing against the old time-to-fill metric. A better approach is to establish an actionable target start date for the new hire, then move backward from that date to schedule your process. Managers need three great candidates to choose from. For this to happen, you need three great candidates to reach the final stages of interviewing simultaneously. *Your timeline will look something like this:*

Week 0	Intake meeting. The job is open. You're building the job description and the scorecard.
Week 1–2	Sourcing on all cylinders. Marketers and sourcers leverage all appropriate channels to attract candidates.
Week 3	Prescreening. Sourcers qualify candidates and build a shortlist.
Week 4	Interviews. 4–6 candidates are in first-round interviews.
Week 5	More interviews. 2–3 candidates return for final interviews.
Week 6	Offer. Selected candidate receives offer, and she accepts—obviously!
Week X	Start. Two weeks later in the US, ten weeks later in Europe, your candidate starts.

Using a target start date sets reasonable expectations and allows for accurate department budgeting. For instance, in Europe you need to plan hires further ahead because the average notice period is fifty-seven days. In this scenario, the third-quarter hiring budget would be approved in the first quarter. In the United States, where the notice period is fourteen days, the third-quarter hiring budget would be approved in the second quarter. Mapping this out ahead of time is critical, as it allows you to organize your hiring plan and meet hiring velocity expectations.

AUTOMATING FOR EXCELLENCE

So, what's the most time-consuming aspect of the recruiting process? Most people naturally assume it's sourcing—not true. The culprit: waiting. You wait for feedback on resumes, wait for interviews to be scheduled, wait for interview feedback to be processed, and wait for an offer to be issued. The waiting goes on and on. Obviously, a dragging process delays hiring, but it also reduces quality. The slower the process, the harder it becomes to attract the best of the best, who get scooped up by competitors.

While the talent acquisition team can do a lot to reduce sourcing times—starting with proper anticipating and pipelining—the overall process cycle time can be greatly optimized through automation and collaboration. With good recruiting software, sourcing is predictable, screening happens on time, the interview slots are prebooked, scheduling is centralized, interview feedback is shared, and the offer process is automated. When recruiters and managers collaborate on a single system, it streamlines the process and cuts out the waste created by trading emails and using spreadsheets.

SHARED SERVICES

Clear operating models allow organizations to consolidate and reach economies of scale by tapping into increased automation. Organizationally, this requires the centralization of the talent acquisition functions into shared services or centers of excellence. The benefits of this structure include centralized marketing and sourcing and a technology team that owns the system from enablement, processes, and insights all the way to privacy and compliance.

The talent acquisition team is the one function that needs to stay close to the business, anticipating the hiring manager's needs and working hand in hand with their trusted colleague to hire great talent on demand.

THE RIGHT FUNDING

Now that you have a good picture of what a modern talent acquisition team looks like, you can drill down on what your talent acquisition budget should be and how to resource your team accordingly. Should you have sixteen recruiters per one thousand employees, like Google, or just two, the average?

As a starting exercise, you might consider spending 8 percent of each candidate's salary on their recruitment—an average investment, according to the Society for Human Resource Management.

Now, let's imagine your company has 1,000 employees, and is growing at a yearly rate of 20 percent (add 200), with 10 percent churn (lose 100). That's about 300 external hires. At an average salary of $50,000, an 8 percent budget represents $4,000 per hire, or $1.2 million total.

With this budget, you would probably allocate 50 percent to technology (talent acquisition suite and add-on systems); third parties (assessment, background checks, etc.); and programs (advertising, referrals, and marketing). The other 50 percent would be allocated to the team. At that scale, you are probably looking at a team of ten. Traditionally, that would likely end up being one leader and nine full-stack jacks-of-all-trades (recruiters, sourcers, coordinators). Instead, I would advocate that by specializing the team, one would get much better outcomes. *If I were assembling a recruiting team to hire a mix of Core, Specialists, Professionals, and Unicorns, I would split my ten-person team as follows:*

- **Director of Talent Acquisition (1):** to lead the team and handle executive recruiting.

- **Recruiting Ops (1):** to manage systems, deliver insights, and drive automation and efficiency.

- **Marketers (2):** to fill the pipeline through advertising (for Core and Professionals) and campaigns (for Specialists and Professionals).

- **Sourcers (2):** to prescreen for some jobs and source outbound for Unicorns and problematic roles.

- **Coordinators (2):** to schedule interviews (at least for Specialists and Unicorns) and preboard all candidates (with a heavy lift from automation).

- **Recruiters (2):** to serve as talent advisors and candidate managers for your company's top one hundred roles only.

The above team, if well chosen, should be efficient at making 300 hires a year for your company. What goes into that? They'll field 3,000 candidates, manage over 150 interviews, make 30 offers, and handle everything in between to close 25 jobs per month.

Whether you commit to an average investment as described above or raise the bar higher depends on your market. Setting targets for hiring velocity (at least 80 percent) and net hiring score (at least +20) will help you determine the appropriate level of funding for your talent acquisition team. And given that top talent is four to eight times more productive than average talent, my guess is that your return on hiring would still look very strong even if you were to double the average recruiting budget. And just for fun, imagine what you could accomplish by investing *eight times more, like Google.*

KEY TAKEAWAYS

- Hiring success requires excellent collaboration between managers and recruiters. This relationship must be strong, or the hiring process will be broken.

- Define clear service levels by talent segment to ensure smooth delivery and appropriate allocation of effort.

- Anticipation denotes intelligence. Great recruiting starts with great planning.

- To scale your talent acquisition function, invest in Rec Ops, automation, and shared services.

CHAPTER 19

WHERE TALENT MEETS TECHNOLOGY

O n January 31, 1999, while the Denver Broncos were busy defeating the Atlanta Falcons in Super Bowl XXXIII to become the new National Football League champions, the world of recruiting suddenly changed. This was the day Monster.com, a small startup company, aired its instantly famous "When I Grow Up" ad.

That thirty-second Super Bowl ad took online recruiting into the mainstream, ushering in the rise of online applications and opening up thousands upon thousands of jobs to a whole new world of candidates.

Around that time, I met Monster's founder, Jeff Taylor, at a conference. I vividly remember hearing him say, "Headhunters have looked at the future. They prefer the past." My stomach sank when he said this. I was a headhunter myself at the time, and I felt I'd just been declared extinct. I began to wonder: *Would I be able to assimilate into this new recruiting world?*

A ROCKY START FOR APPLICANT TRACKING SYSTEMS

I laid awake that night thinking about jobs and applicants and realized that if recruiting was going online, companies would need an applicant tracking system. The next morning, my decision was made: I would form a recruiting software company of my own. Fast-forward six months, and my co-founder and I, backed by $30 million in venture capital, were off to the races to build one of the industry's first applicant tracking systems. I called our ATS MrTed (don't ask me where that name came from).

Big-name companies like Siemens, Heineken, France Telecom, and Danone jumped aboard and started using the software. And soon enough, we were processing more than three million applications monthly.

Unfortunately, I got it all wrong. Like the dozen or so other companies working in the ATS field at that time (think Taleo, BrassRing, and iCIMS), I was thinking too small. At the time, recruiting departments were essentially giant piles of paper resumes with no tracking capabilities. So the problem MrTed and our competitors solved for was paper processing. Far from revolutionizing recruiting, we'd settled for replacing the file cabinet with record keeping software.

Not surprisingly, the leader of the ATS market ended up being Taleo (later acquired by Oracle), founded by Louis Tetu. Tetu was the former president of Baan SCS, a company that designs factory production systems. With Taleo, he applied supply-chain efficiency models to recruiting—moving applicants through the hiring process like products on an assembly line.

This is not what recruiting is about! Hiring success is about finding candidates, choosing the right ones, and staying organized.

And yet, here we are, twenty years later. Can you guess which ATS is still the market leader? That's right, it's Taleo. The software is so ineffective that a recent Change.org petition called for Larry Ellison, the CEO of Oracle, to shut it down.

While some companies *are* changing their ATS, their attempted improvements aren't always contributing to hiring success. In many cases, the recruiting system is now subsumed into an even larger human resource information system (HRIS) such as Oracle, SAP, or Workday. Unfortunately, these HRISs are designed for record-keeping, not candidate attraction, user experience, or collaboration. No wonder so many recruiters and hiring managers simply refuse to use these systems to manage recruiting—and CEOs continue to lament that they aren't hiring the best talent.

Does your ATS facilitate hiring success for your company? Just think about it, and ask yourself the following simple questions:

- Does my ATS help me find and engage great candidates? (No. It was designed to track them, not find them. It's a record-keeper, not a marketing tool.)

- Do managers use my ATS every day to manage their hiring? (No. It was not designed for collaboration with managers. As a result, the process is managed offline.)

- Does my ATS make my recruiters happy and productive? (No. They can't run modern recruiting on an outdated database, so most of the activity happens offline in emails and spreadsheets. It's inefficient and not compliant.)

Did I correctly anticipate your answers to those questions? I'm guessing so. Applicant tracking systems simply do not deliver hiring success. And that is what compelled me to create the next generation of the modern talent acquisition suite.

WHAT A MODERN TALENT ACQUISITION SUITE DELIVERS

When my ATS company, MrTed, was acquired in 2010, I had a tough choice to make: take two years off to sail around the world, or go build the next generation of recruiting software. I opted for the latter. There were too many jobs open, too many people looking for work, and too many companies struggling to hire. Connecting people to jobs at scale was one technology problem I thought I had a shot at solving.

Eight years and $100 million in venture capital later, SmartRecruiters has built a modern and enterprise-grade global talent acquisition suite that delivers hiring success for hundreds of companies and millions of candidates around the world. What I learned in this journey is that talent acquisition technology really has become very similar to the tech stack that sales and marketing departments have been using for a decade. Most importantly, I've learned that whether a company decides to invest in a full technology suite or assemble point solutions on top of their HRIS or ATS to solve niche issues, a successful software solution must, at bare minimum, possess the following three attributes.

DESIGNED TO ATTRACT CANDIDATES

Job number one for the talent acquisition suite should be to help you bring in great candidates. Just as a modern marketing platform brings in prospective customers, you will need functionalities to attract, engage, nurture, and convert candidates. That means your talent acquisition suite should have all of your recruitment marketing tools in one place—career site, job advertising, content marketing, direct sourcing, referrals, field events, and so on—while facilitating an amazing, on-brand candidate experience from first touch to hire.

MANAGERS LOVE IT

As discussed in the previous chapter, collaboration between recruiters and hiring managers is the number-one indicator of high-performance recruiting. This means that managers (and interviewers) need to be using the talent acquisition suite virtually every day to work with the recruiters in an effective way. If they don't, the process will go back to running on emails and spreadsheets, which is both inefficient and noncompliant. So, your talent acquisition suite should be built mobile-first, accessible from anywhere, anytime, on any device, while facilitating objective interview feedback and effortless collaboration between the hiring team and recruiters. It puzzles me when I see large companies selecting a new recruiting solution without evaluating the experience of other key stakeholders—managers in particular.

MAKES RECRUITERS PRODUCTIVE

Talent acquisition teams have a challenging role. They are effectively operating a full-scale sales and marketing function with a fraction of the resources. To do their job well, they need their core technology, the talent acquisition suite, to be a source of truth and a system of record. It must enable the entire process, from early-stage pipelining all the way to onboarding. The talent acquisition team cannot perform at a high level if they have ten different tools with tracking results strewn across multiple spreadsheets. Thus, all data, processes, activities, and suppliers must meet in one system that allows the team to be in control, compliant, and productive.

In summary, your talent acquisition suite must facilitate the principles of hiring success: candidate experience, manager engagement, and recruiter productivity.

Now, from a systems perspective, your IT team is likely to weigh in with their own requirements. They usually include the following.

BUILT-IN FLEXIBILITY

Recruiting is by nature a fluid process that adapts to market conditions and to the specifics of each job. The way we source and hire engineers is very different from the way we hire salespeople or interns or executives. What's different? Almost everything, from where we find candidates, to the questions we ask upon application, to the prescreening criteria, the interview scorecard, the number of interviews, the assessments we use, and the approvals we need. Unlike other HR processes, such as the "annual performance review" or "vacation approval," recruiting cannot be forced into a single, rigid, preconfigured workflow. That's why HRISs and ATSs have struggled to gain user adoption. These tools simply don't do what recruiters and managers need them to. Savvy IT buyers understand that, and will request a software that can support multiple processes, workflows, and automations—right down to the individual job.

GLOBALLY LOCAL

Most cloud-based enterprise systems nowadays are expected to operate globally. The challenge with recruiting is that while you are operating a global recruiting function, each job is actually local. The talent acquisition suite needs to support local recruiting in each of the countries you operate in globally. What does that mean? To start, it needs to support local language—Chinese people apply to jobs in Chinese—and to be compliant with local regulations. Did you know it's actually illegal to post a job in English in France, or to ask diversity questions in Germany? Beyond that, the talent acquisition suite needs to support recruiting channels in each country.

LinkedIn is popular in the U.S., but WeChat is where people job-hunt in China, and Xing still claims a large market share in Germany while Seek dominates in Australia. The bottom line: unlike most other HR processes, recruiting needs to be globally local, not just global. This is typically a challenge for HRIS/ATS systems.

PREINTEGRATED WITH *EVERYTHING*

Recruiting is a market-facing function that needs to leverage many different services and vendors. Think: job boards (Stepstone, Monster, Seek, Glassdoor); social networks (LinkedIn, Facebook, Twitter, WeChat); search engines (Indeed, Google). Then there's your own website, personality assessment vendors, skills testing platforms, reference checks, background checks. And of course, the countless new technologies on the market (chatbots, artificial-intelligence matching, automated sourcing, candidate engagement, and data management, to name a few). The average SmartRecruiters enterprise customer leverages integrations to twenty-three other services and vendors. Understandably, from an IT perspective, your talent acquisition suite should be preintegrated with all of these external services. If it is not, your integration and maintenance costs—not to mention the pain of managing a disjointed system—will explode.

If your company is in the early stages of deciding whether to use the recruiting module of your HR system or bring in a modern talent acquisition suite, no doubt you can look forward to some lively conversations. But first, let's talk about compliance and privacy.

ARE YOU COMPLIANT?

In addition to its functional and technical requirements, the talent acquisition suite must address the complex issue of compliance. Recruiting is a heavily regulated industry, and with good reason—or at least good intention. Every country (or state) has its local flavor, along with unique rules about where companies can advertise, the questions they are allowed to ask candidates, and so on. In New York, for example, it's illegal to ask a candidate about their current salary, but it's fine in Michigan, for now.

Sometimes the rules can get quirky. For example, in the event of a tie between candidates applying to work for the U.S. Federal Government, the last digit of the Social Security number of each candidate will be multiplied by a randomly generated number to determine who gets hired.

To make a long story short, having a solid talent acquisition suite that is the system of record and the single source of truth for all things recruiting ensures that you always stay on the right side of the law. And that is especially true when considering data privacy.

DATA PRIVACY

Over the last few years, data privacy has become a headline topic. Since the implementation of the General Data Protection Regulation (GDPR) in Europe, other countries and states including China, Russia, Australia, and California have all issued new and more restrictive privacy regulations. What do these regulations look like?

In general, they offer more protection and control for data subjects (candidates) to ensure that the data controller (employer) and their data processor (the talent acquisition suite) only store relevant data (the candidate's resume) for a single purpose (applying for a particular job), and for a limited duration (until the candidate is rejected or hired). And of course, none of this should happen without the candidate's consent.

Think about that for a minute. Talent acquisition teams are in the business of accumulating private data. It's no secret that inside most organizations, resumes are floating around everywhere, shared between staff, and comments about candidates are emailed all over the place. All of this is in breach of the GDPR in Europe, and the fines are serious—up to 5 percent of company revenue. Even worse, a breach doesn't need to be exposed through a government body; any candidate can raise a claim (including any of the hundreds or thousands that you didn't hire and forgot to respond to). It's no wonder that one of the largest global consultancy companies recently assigned a team to build an algorithm to sift through the email inboxes of its employees to identify and delete resumes.

Certainly, complying with privacy laws can be a tangled and intimidating endeavor. But it doesn't have to be. You just need to establish a workable system—by which I mean a single system. All (and I mean *all*) recruiting activity must happen in one system where you can enforce proper controls, consent, and retention policies. Compliance is another compelling reason why having managers and interviewers use the same system as recruiters is so critical.

So, with all of this in mind, which system should you pick? Will it be an HRIS, or a talent acquisition suite?

THE MODERN TA SUITE VERSUS THE ALL-IN-ONE HRIS

Human resource information systems like those offered by Workday, SAP, and Oracle roll recruiting, human resources, payroll, management, and accounting functions into one heavyweight package.

While the idea of an all-in-one platform may sound appealing at first, many companies ultimately recognize that the unique nature of recruiting as a fluid sales and marketing function differs from rigid and internal-facing HR processes—and thus it demands something different.

As you assess the best course of action for your company, here are a few angles to evaluate:

- **Recruiting outcomes:** Which approach will best serve your talent acquisition team and the company in achieving hiring success—attracting, selecting, and hiring amazing talent on demand?

- **IT simplicity:** Which option will be easiest for your IT team to manage? At the outset, it may seem that the one-system HRIS approach is easier. But will that hold true when the IT team is eventually asked to address evolving processes, localized workflows, and dozens of integrations? IT may choose to ignore such requests for a period of time, during which hiring performance will suffer. Is that the right trade-off?

- **Data privacy:** To manage data privacy properly, the legal and compliance officer will require that all recruiting activity is contained within one system. From their perspective, any system is acceptable provided that all candidate data is in one place where recruiters, managers, and interviewers can collaborate. If the managers aren't using the system, then that is a big red flag for privacy.

- **Security:** The fourth perspective, which I have been seeing more and more, is that of the information security officer. When it comes to security, recruiting software is naturally a vulnerability, given that it is exposed to the cloud and aims at bringing external people (candidates) into the company. Therefore, security will say that recruiting needs to be placed in a demilitarized zone (DMZ) that must be partitioned outside of core HR data. In the event of data breaches, this system architecture prevents penetration of and access to core, and perhaps more sensitive, HR data. From this perspective, keeping the talent acquisition suite separate from HRIS is becoming a popular information security strategy.

I am of course biased in this argument, given that I've dedicated the last decade to building a talent acquisition suite. But I do believe that your choice between HRIS and a talent acquisition suite is about whether you want a marketing tool or a record-keeping tool. Your HRIS system is designed to keep records of your employees and manage employee lifecycle workflows. Your talent acquisition suite is a marketing and collaboration tool designed to help you compete for the best talent. (Once candidates are hired, the recruiting system will automatically pass the candidate on to HRIS/payroll through one integration.)

The logistics of recruiting have changed immensely since the days of paper resumes. Are you equipped for the new era, or stuck in the past? If we are indeed in a global battle for talent, it might be time to hit the front lines.

KEY TAKEAWAYS

- Applicant tracking systems (ATS) were not designed to attract candidates and deliver hiring success. They need to be replaced.

- Likewise, the recruiting module of your human resources and payroll system is not a talent acquisition suite and won't deliver hiring success.

- A modern talent acquisition suite is a candidate attraction engine that boosts productivity for recruiters—and that managers *love* using.

- Recruiting software must be highly flexible, preintegrated with all your vendors, and globally local to support complex recruiting processes.

- Compliance and data privacy are growing concerns that need to be handled very seriously.

CHAPTER 20

DIVERSITY IS
THE CAKE

grew up surrounded by nature. As a child in Northern France, I would lie in the tall grass of the fields around my home and contemplate the sky, the clouds, and the beauty all around me. Birds swooped by, insects crawled up blades of grass, flowers and trees bent with the breeze. They were all interconnected, a minute sample of the estimated 8.7 million plant and animal species that form Earth's biodiversity. The breadth of our planetary diversity has awed and fascinated me ever since. Nature, when you think about it, is an endlessly complex and extraordinary organization. As each component strives toward perfection, it plays a part in the greater evolution of the system.

Although all 7.5 billion humans on Earth share a four-letter genetic code, and we all descend from the same one thousand migrants who left Africa some fifty thousand years ago, the human race is extraordinarily diverse in so many ways: gender, ethnicity, race, class, religion, nationality, sexuality, philosophy, and lifestyle. The biological and cultural diversity that has risen from our remarkable adaptability is beautiful.

This human diversity is what allows us to continue to evolve and adapt in our daily lives—and in the workplace, too. Diversity is in fact exactly what businesses need to thrive. Just as biodiversity is necessary to sustain natural habitats and ecosystems, human diversity is the core fabric of long-term corporate sustainability and performance. Our strength lies in our differences, not our similarities.

WHY DIVERSITY MATTERS

Workplace diversity is defined as understanding, accepting, and valuing differences between people of different genders, races, ethnicities, sexual orientations, ages, abilities, and religions—as well as differences in personality, skillset, education, and experiences.

Why does diversity matter? Well, imagine you're heading into a trivia-night competition, where questions on a vast range of topics will be put to team players. Who would make up your ideal team? It seems evident that your chances of winning would increase if your team members had different backgrounds, experiences, ages, and interests.

The same is true in the workplace. Research shows that organizations comprised of a wide range of age and geographical groups make better business decisions 87 percent of the time. Similarly, cognitively diverse teams are shown to solve problems faster than teams made up of cognitively similar people.[38] And if there was any question about the value of gender and ethnic diversity in the workplace, a recent McKinsey & Company study found that businesses with high gender diversity on the executive team were 21 percent more likely to experience above-average profitability than companies with low gender diversity; and ethnically diverse executive teams were 33 percent more likely than ethnically homogenous teams to outperform their competition.

IF DIVERSITY IS GOOD FOR BUSINESS, WHY DON'T WE EMBRACE IT?

Why don't we embrace diversity? Let's start with the fact that 95 percent of CEOs of S&P 500 companies are white men. Sad but true. In fact, did you know that there are more CEOs named David (4.5 percent) than there are women CEOs (4.1

---

38 Forbes, 2017.

percent)?[39] These men at the top of the corporate ladder don't always embrace diversity because, well, that's human nature. Our nature is to surround ourselves with people who think like us and look like us—not to engage with, let alone hire, people who are different. So, we discriminate consciously and unconsciously through our actions, our processes, and ultimately through the very fabric of our society. Thirty-three percent of African Americans hold at least a two-year college degree,[40] yet multicultural professionals—including black, Hispanic, and Asian Americans—collectively hold only 14 percent of senior executive and manager positions in corporate America.[41] This is a systemic problem that can and should be solved through hiring, training, and internal promotion within corporations. The good news is: we're working on it. Over the last three years, hiring for jobs in the diversity and inclusion department has increased by 35 percent, and it's now common for executive teams to include a vice president of diversity and inclusion.

But we're only just getting started, and the road ahead of us—toward a future where truly diverse workplaces are the rule, not the exception—is long. How will we get there?

---

39 Harvard Business Review, 2016.
40 The Postsecondary National Policy Institute, 2019.
41 Inc., 2018.

EXTREME MEASURES

How can we increase workplace diversity? Sometimes, extreme circumstances justify extreme measures. In 1991, when Nelson Mandela was elected president of the African National Congress, he had to turn around decades of Apartheid. He quickly passed the Black Economic Empowerment Laws, which addressed the inequities of Apartheid by forcing South African businesses to diversify their workforce and management. As an example, businesses had to ensure that 60 percent of management-level seats were filled with black employees, and they were given bonus points for compliance when they hired female employees. While the BEE Laws continue to be controversial to this day, they undoubtedly led to improved diversity in the country's business sector, not to mention the creation of a black middle class in South Africa.

I do believe that diversity in hiring must be at the top of every executive's agenda. Fortunately, meaningful progress toward this goal can be made by taking three simple steps: sourcing diverse candidates, reducing bias in the recruitment phase, and building inclusion.

SOURCING DIVERSITY

A tech entrepreneur friend of mine was complaining recently about how hard it was for him to find and hire female engineers. Digging into the problem for him, I went to the career page on his website. At the top of the page was the job ad for software developers, reading: "Ninja rock star wanted to dominate our market." I turned to my daughter, who happens to enjoy her computer programming classes at school, and asked her, "Would you apply?" She raised one eyebrow in response— teenager code for "yeah, no way." Diversity sourcing starts with making diverse candidates feel wanted and welcome. And that starts with the language you use in your job description. Gender-specific language is obviously a no-go. Instead, the language you choose should be respectful and inclusive, kind and compassionate, mindful and empowering. In a single word: humanizing.

As you think through your employer brand, always consider what is the best way to showcase your commitment to diversity and inclusion. Who will take note? The younger generation, your ideal candidate pool, who care deeply about social justice. Approximately half of men and women surveyed said they had researched their company's diversity and inclusion policy before accepting their job. And still more employees assessed the diversity of their company's leadership team before signing on.[42]

It certainly makes good sense to take a hard look at your talent attraction strategies through the lens of diversity. What does your team do to extend your reach beyond the norm? Do they advertise for candidates at diverse colleges? Partner with professional associations that support underrepresented communities? Insist on the importance of diversity in your referral program? All of these practices require minimal expense and effort, yet can drive significant progress toward the diverse workforce your company deserves.

There are many overlooked sources of talent. For example, the vast majority of the 2.7 million United States military service members who served in Iraq and Afghanistan over the past two decades are now back home, with many in need of employment. And each year, more than 650,000 people are released from U.S. prisons. They, too, comprise a valuable talent pool. I know this because I volunteer at Pelican Bay, a maximum-security prison in California. The men I work with there have committed serious crimes, and most are serving multidecade terms. Yet, they have incredible skills—as well as resilience, depth, and compassion. I would hire many of them in a heartbeat. The formerly incarcerated

---

42 LinkedIn Global Recruiting Trends, 2018.

population represents a large and diverse pool of talent that shouldn't be ignored.

REDUCING BIAS IN SCREENING

Even before a candidate's first interview, bias can be working against them—triggered by the name on their resume. In a BBC study on the phenomenon of name bias, two resumes with identical experiences, education, and skillsets were placed on four job sites and submitted in response to two hundred job listings. The results: "Adam Henton" was offered three times more job interviews than "Mohamed Allam."

Name and address discrimination is so bad that, in 2006, the French government passed a law to allow candidates to apply to jobs anonymously. Alas, the idea of an "anonymous resume" was hard to implement and had mixed effects. The law was subsequently struck down, and the problem remains in most every country.

So, how do you reduce the chance that name bias is influencing your team's hiring decisions? One approach might sound extreme: let a computer take the first pass at screening resumes. When machines are employed to select or reject resumes based solely on objective data like skill, experience, and education, the problem can be greatly diminished. Today, algorithms created through machine analysis of hundreds of millions of career-relevant criteria are already effectively eliminating a host of bias-related issues at many companies.

Another way to reduce bias is to use standardized testing. Coding candidates can demonstrate their skills on a testing platform rather than submit a resume, thus eliminating institutional bias. If a programmer can show she knows Python backwards and forwards, why should it matter if she went to Stanford or learned coding on YouTube? Whether through AI resume screening or testing for objective skills, technology is an excellent tool to reduce screening bias. It's so successful, in fact, that the state of California recently passed the Fair Recruiting Act, which urges companies to employ digital solutions for fairer screening.

It's not just about including one diverse candidate on your candidate shortlist, of course. If there is only one woman, minority, or differently-abled person on that list, they will have little chance of being hired. As one study found, on a shortlist of three candidates, people usually pick one from the majority. If there are two males and a female candidate, a male gets hired, and vice versa. This goes for any "different" candidate—e.g., if there are two white candidates and one black candidate, the white person will be hired, and vice versa.[43] If you're serious

---

43 Harvard Business Review, 2016.

about increasing diversity at your company, ensure that your talent acquisition team is building applicant shortlists that give those diverse candidates their fairest shot.

REDUCING BIAS IN INTERVIEWING

So, your diverse candidates have made the first cut—great job. Now it's time to remove bias from your interview process, which is highly susceptible to unconscious bias in particular. I learned this firsthand a couple of years ago at SmartRecruiters as we were interviewing a candidate for a senior sales role. He had the perfect profile. Been there, done that. Ambitious. Your typical white male software sales guy. Our interview team was comprised of three men and two women. All three men, including me, rated the guy four or five stars; we were ready to go. The two women, on the other hand, gave him two stars. Both shared remarkably similar feedback: in their eyes, the candidate was disrespectful, a bully. "This is not who we are," one of the women said. And just like that, we avoided what would surely have been a costly hiring mistake, causing an inevitable disruption within the team.

In order to consistently reduce bias in interviewing, I recommend using a combination of three things: a diverse interview team, a structured scorecard, and radical transparency. The magic trifecta.

A DIVERSE INTERVIEW TEAM

In chapter 13, we discussed the ways that team interviewing in a structured format can root out bias and improve results. To further amplify these benefits, your interview teams should be as diverse as possible. Since we humans prefer people who think and look like us, and human nature is hard to change, this makes good sense. Remember, diverse teams make better decisions 87 percent of the time.

AN OBJECTIVE, STRUCTURED SCORECARD

Once your diverse interview team is assembled, you can help them remain neutral by keeping the interview focused around your structured scorecard, which has been created for the job. This structure narrows the option for unconscious bias and forces a fair evaluation based on what actually matters—that objective criteria.

RADICAL TRANSPARENCY

Scorecards now in hand, will your interviewers actually speak their mind and give unbiased feedback? The answer is yes, if they are using the "cards down" approach. That is, an interviewer cannot see others' evaluations before he has submitted his own. At that point, the team should absolutely share and discuss their ratings. Discrimination thrives behind closed doors, after all. Nobody wants to publicly discriminate. It's only with radical candor that objective decisions will be made.

BUILD INCLUSION

It's one thing to be invited to a party. It's another to be invited to dance. Diversity without inclusion is meaningless. Unfortunately, the recruiting process is designed for *exclusion*—the separation of the "good" from the "bad." Changing this process will take you out of your comfort zone, but it can be done.

For example, for individuals who are somewhere on the autism spectrum, the interview process presents a significant barrier. It doesn't work for a person with autism to be grilled in a formal interview. That's just not an effective way to assess their amazing skills. Recognizing this, Microsoft does not hold traditional interviews for candidates with autism. Instead, these candidates are invited to spend two weeks on campus working on actual projects while being casually monitored by managers looking for new team members. That's inclusion.

Another company taking radical steps to ensure a fair hiring process is New York's Greyston Bakery, where the motto is: "We don't hire people to bake brownies, we bake brownies to hire people." Having practiced open hiring for thirty years, Greyston's selection criteria are crystal clear: they have none.

As a candidate, if you think you can do the job, you write your name on a signup sheet and show up to work the next day. No interview, no questions. Self-selection: that's inclusive.

When it comes to assessing underrepresented candidates, sometimes all you need to do is meet them. Rather than screening them in a process, just talk to them—connect with them as human beings. This is often the best way to discover their hidden talents, their passion, their creativity, and all the things they could bring to your organization. If only they were given this opportunity more often.

Earlier this year at SmartRecruiters, we launched a large-scale initiative we call Reverse Recruiting. The principle is simple: on Reverse Recruiting days (usually a Friday afternoon once a quarter), recruiters and hiring managers work for the candidates instead of for the company. Invited to participate are people who struggle to find work—people who are normally excluded from job opportunities by design. Our recruiters and managers spend the afternoon advising their guests on the job market, interview strategies, and other aspects of the job search.

Reverse recruiting has gone so well at SmartRecruiters that we recently tried it at one of our Hiring Success conferences in Amsterdam. In the room were four hundred recruiting leaders who cumulatively make about a million hires a year. We surprised them by inviting four hundred candidates into the room. These candidates were people who could greatly benefit from connecting with the professionals in that room, so we connected them. For the next two hours, our paying conference attendees forged connections with candidates whom the traditional interviewing process is designed to reject, whether because they were differently-abled, gender nonconforming, formerly incarcerated, senior citizens, refugees, or lacking housing. It was beautiful to witness corporate recruiters being moved, opening up, and finally being in a position to include rather than exclude.

What makes us human? Seeing the beauty in our differences. If we can bring that humanity to our hiring processes, we can become better leaders, build better companies, and help rebalance inequity. Who we hire defines the world we want to live in.

KEY TAKEAWAYS

- Workplace diversity is defined as understanding, accepting, and valuing differences between people of different races, ethnicities, genders, ages, religions, abilities, and sexual orientations—as well as differences in personality, skillset, education, and experience.

- Just as biodiversity is necessary to sustain natural habitats and ecosystems, human diversity is the core fabric of long-term corporate sustainability and performance.

- Progress toward workplace diversity can be made by taking three steps: sourcing diverse candidates, reducing bias in the recruitment phase, and building inclusion.

- The magical trifecta to reduce bias in interviewing: a diverse interview team, a structured scorecard, and radical transparency.

- What makes us human? Seeing the beauty in our differences.

CHAPTER 21

THE FUTURE OF HIRING SUCCESS

L ast summer, I hosted members of the SmartRecruiters product and engineering teams for an off-site retreat. The agenda was to brainstorm about what we wanted recruiting to look like in 2030. How would technology help us achieve our mission to connect people with jobs at scale?

So, there we were, at an eco-friendly seaside lodge outside of Amsterdam—fifteen people who have devoted much of our careers and brainpower to understanding how technology can help solve recruiting.

The bulk of our discussion revolved around how technology will help employers navigate the growing global skills shortage (discussed in chapter 1). Most of the group felt optimistic that corporations of the future would rise to the challenges brought by more competition. We all agreed that the ability to attract and hire the best people will become the primary competitive differentiator across all industries.

By 2030, access to abundant capital and technology will be a given. All organizations will be competing with the same tools. The only real differentiator will be people. And so this competitive pressure will drive recruiting toward perfection as an economic market. In other words, the labor market will be more fluid and transparent, driving search friction down and the speed and quality of recruiting transactions up.

Sound optimistic? Not really. Much of this has already started to happen.

Markets become fluid when search friction (how long it takes for supply and demand to meet in the job market) and transaction costs (the effort and expenses required to transact) go down. And technology is obviously the primary catalyst for disruption. Think about what Airbnb did for the short-term vacation rental market. Before Airbnb, imagine the difficulty of booking an apartment for the weekend in Moscow—from across the globe. It would have been a massive headache to find the right place (search friction), sign a rental contract, and wire funds to the owner (transaction costs). Today, it takes a few clicks. The same is bound to happen in the recruiting space, as data becomes more reliable and available and transaction costs continue to fall, thanks to automation.

So, let's look more closely at the future of data availability and reliability.

THE END OF THE RESUME

When you think about it, the current practice of sharing resumes, or curriculum vitae (CVs), from our personal desktops is quite inefficient. The document is available only to the handful of people it's sent to, and it contains limited—and often inaccurate and unverified—information. Instead of keeping a CV on their desktop, job candidates of the future will share their employment history via an online document. The universal profile will contain everything a potential employer needs to know about the candidate's education, employment history, personality type, and job preferences. All of this information, including employer references, actual skills, and personality attributes, will be prevalidated and secured by blockchain, so only prospective employers can have access.

REPUTATION IS EVERYTHING

Until recently, there has been no meaningful way, beyond the verbiage on corporate websites, for prospective candidates to obtain accurate information about employers. Luckily, this is changing. Thanks to the Glassdoor effect, every company's culture and recruiting process is increasingly transparent. In the next decade, candidates will have instant access to a vast array of public information on every employer, including manager ratings, diversity ratings, benefits breakdowns, culture assessments, response rates, and overall candidate experience. Needless to say, employer brand and reputation will be of paramount importance. Without it, companies won't have access to talent.

With accurate and reliable data available on both sides, plus ever-growing levels of intelligence and automation, the matching of candidates to jobs will become easier and easier.

MY PERSONAL AI HEADHUNTER

As matching algorithms become increasingly accurate, we will likely see the emergence of a new sort of job-search solution— the personal AI headhunter. This resource will be every candidate's best friend. The AI will be constantly on the lookout for new opportunities for its human. It will know the job market so well that it will be able to predict job openings on the horizon and steer the candidate toward the best fits. It will apply and manage the application process on behalf of the candidate, freeing up their time and energy.

AUTOMATED SOURCING

On the corporate side, sourcing automation has already started and will continue to accelerate. AI-powered sourcing tools will advertise jobs automatically, find candidate matches, and reach out to those with the most relevant profiles through their phone or their own AI headhunter. Like a true marketer, the corporate AI sourcer will even reengage past candidates and existing employees to sell them on new opportunities. It will diligently follow up when appropriate and offer to schedule initial conversations as a first step—since applying to jobs and initial prescreening won't be necessary anymore.

You might be starting to wonder: *Is this really such good news?* I think so. For candidates, a more transparent job market means better pay and better access to desirable jobs, which drives better behaviors and happiness. Anyone who's *not* happy in their job can easily change. Most, though, will stay at their company longer and longer, thanks to their enlightened, conscientious employers.

As for those employers, they'll be thriving, too. Why wouldn't they? The new, low-friction job market will mean more jobs are created, unemployment is low, and the economy is thriving. It's a better world for everyone.

On this journey toward hiring success, I only hope we will strive to increase diversity in the workplace and society overall. Who we hire defines the world we want to live in.

You are who you hire.

ACKNOWLEDGMENTS

Writing this book was super easy, and I have a lot of people to thank for that.

First off, special thanks to my team: Elodie Lang for making my life blissful always, Genevieve Field for allowing to tell my story, Henrietta Johnston for your amazing research, Jack Wei for your relentless commitment to make this happen, and Rebecca Carr for your inspiration and ability to move mountains. Without all of you, this book would not have been written.

I am so grateful for the amazing team at SmartRecruiters. To all the Smartians: thank you for joining me on this journey to match people to jobs at scale. Particular thanks (in order of appearance) to Rafal, Charlie, Michal, Natalia, Daniel, Rebecca, Anna, Roy, MJ, Alison, Rob, Eric, Prachi, Bob, Hessam, Robin,

Valerie, Sarah, Dave, and Christian. You have given me the opportunity to redefine what great recruiting looks like, and you make me a better leader every day.

Thank you to the product managers, designers, and our engineering teams—Foo Fighters, 42, Zoo, Mob, Null Pointers, Data Bandits, Space Invaders, Tycoons, Everest—who make my dreams come true through amazing software. Special thoughts for Margaux, Kelly, Jakub, Dipti, Shefali, Jan, Manuel, and Jason.

Thank you to my investors, in particular Rajeev Batra at Mayfield for believing in me early on, and Matt Gatto and Jeff Liebermann at Insight for fueling our growth. Your partnership has been invaluable. Special thanks to Brett Queener for…everything :-).

Thank you to the thousands of talent acquisition leaders who have partnered with SmartRecruiters to make hiring easy. Special thoughts to the teams at Visa, Bosch, Ikea, Square, Equinox, Avery Dennison, Twitter, Expeditors, Publicis, CERN, Foster Farms, Ubisoft, LinkedIn, and Skechers. We look forward to continuing the journey to hiring success.

Special thoughts for the EITs and Mavericks at Pelican Bay, for my friends at PBVA. You made me a better person.

And very special thoughts for my early co-founders, Amaury Eloy in Prague, and Frederic Trinel (aka MrFred turned MrTed) in London. Through our experience together, I've come to enjoy roller coasters. Ah, the entrepreneur's life...

And finally, a heartfelt thank you to the two million people who use SmartRecruiters monthly to open a new chapter of their lives. We will continue to fight to make your job search easy.

ABOUT THE AUTHOR

Jerome Ternynck is on a mission to connect people to jobs at scale and remove friction in the labor market. He is an entrepreneur with his heart in recruiting and soul in technology who currently serves as founder and CEO of Silicon Valley-based SmartRecruiters, a global talent acquisition suite rated as the most strategic provider by industry analysts. Jerome has thirty years of experience building award-winning enterprise recruiting software, during which time he pioneered applicant tracking systems and achieved three successful exits. He is recognized as a thought leader in the industry and has been named a top HRTech influencer year after year.

CPSIA information can be obtained
at www.ICGtesting.com
Printed in the USA
JSHW042022290421
14144JS00001B/2